AVIARIES
A COMPLETE INTRODUCTION

——Dr. Matthew M. Vriends——

Owl Finch (*Poephila bichenovii*)

AVIARIES

A COMPLETE INTRODUCTION

—Dr. Matthew M. Vriends—

Red-browed Finch (Aegintha temporalis)

Photographs: C. Allen; Dr. Herbert R. Axelrod; Courtesy of Bird Photographs Inc.; Horst Bielfeld; Joshua Charap & Herschel Frey; Terry Dunham; Tom Gardner; E. Goldfinger; Michael W. Gos; Ray Hanson; Dr. Jesse; Paul Kwast; Harry V. Lacey; P. Leysen; Dan Martin; Louise Van der Meid; H. Muller; A. Van der Nieuwenhuizen; Mervin F. Roberts; L. Robinson; Courtesy of San Diego Zoo; H. Schrempp; W. A. Starika; Courtesy of Vogelpark Walsrode; Dr. M. Vriends; Wayne Wallace.

Based on *Starting an Aviary*.

(t.f.h.)

Distributed in the UNITED STATES by T.F.H. Publications, Inc., 211 West Sylvania Avenue, Neptune City, NJ 07753; in CANADA to the Pet Trade by H & L Pet Supplies Inc., 27 Kingston Crescent, Kitchener, Ontario N2B 2T6; Rolf C. Hagen Ltd., 3225 Sartelon Street, Montreal 382 Quebec; in CANADA to the Book Trade by Macmillan of Canada (A Division of Canada Publishing Corporation), 164 Commander Boulevard, Agincourt, Ontario M1S 3C7; in ENGLAND by T.F.H. Publications Limited, 4 Kier Park, Ascot, Berkshire SL5 7DS; in AUSTRALIA AND THE SOUTH PACIFIC by T.F.H. (Australia) Pty. Ltd., Box 149, Brookvale 2100 N.S.W., Australia; in NEW ZEALAND by Ross Haines & Son, Ltd., 18 Monmouth Street, Grey Lynn, Auckland 2, New Zealand; in SINGAPORE AND MALAYSIA by MPH Distributors (S) Pte., Ltd., 601 Sims Drive, #03/07/21, Singapore 1438; in the PHILIPPINES by Bio-Research, 5 Lippay Street, San Lorenzo Village, Makati Rizal; in SOUTH AFRICA by Multipet Pty. Ltd., 30 Turners Avenue, Durban 4001. Published by T.F.H. Publications, Inc. Manufactured in the United States of America by T.F.H. Publications, Inc.

Contents

Introduction

The goal of this book is to present as concise a picture as possible of the currently very popular bird fancy. A great deal of attention has been devoted to the setting up of the aviary and the daily maintenance and care of its inhabitants, because it is clear that a beginning fancier can certainly use some help in this regard. Making a good start is all-important in avoiding a fiasco later. This is why we have attempted to give detailed information regarding the necessary aspects of the bird fancy, using easy-to-understand language, so that the beginning aviculturist will know which guidelines to follow in order to achieve success with this hobby.

Salmon-crested Cockatoo (Cacatua moluccensis)

A great number of bird species are also fully described, so that the fancier can make a wise decision in his choice of birds.

While reading through the pages, you will realize that keeping birds in your home or garden is a source of pleasure for both young and old, providing they are kept in a responsible manner. We hope and expect that this book will be found useful by a great many fanciers.

I would like to thank Mrs. Terry Williams-Parent and my wife, Mrs. Lucy Vriends-Parent, for their invaluable assistance in the preparation of this edition.

Dr. Matthew M. Vriends

AVIARY CONSTRUCTION

It is not our intention, of course, to give endless details and a blueprint for building an aviary; everyone will build his aviary according to his own ideas—and funds! We do feel it is wise, however, to list several general guide-lines to keep in mind when building one.

OUTDOOR AVIARY

When we visit bird fanciers, it becomes obvious to us that nine out of ten aviaries consist of two or sometimes three parts: a night shelter, a half-open part (with the top being covered with a sheet of corrugated fiberglass or similar material) and an open area, which is called the 'flight.' An aviary consisting of just two parts would lack the covered section of the flight.

Personally, we believe that an aviary consisting of three parts is the most effective. If we can now choose a good location for our aviary, we will be a good distance on the road to success. One of the requirements of the location is that the front of the aviary should face south if at all possible. If this is completely out of the question, then we should have the front face as near to south as possible, favoring southeast rather than southwest. We are also well advised to use

An aviary housing doves and cockatiels. Shades are rolled down during inclement weather to serve as a windbreak.

Aviaries can be designed to fit your needs and available space.

glass in constructing part of the front (not plate glass) and this is certainly necessary if the front does not face south. Apart from this one requirement with regard to the location of the aviary, we should also try to pick a pretty place, preferably where flowers, bushes and trees will frame the aviary, rather than have it standing alone looking rather forlorn with nothing around it. The whole idea is to create as natural an effect as possible.

Which materials should we use? Unless you tend to move often, it is not a good idea to build your aviary from wood alone. The foundation can be made of concrete, which we pour with the upstanding 2 x 4's, metal poles or T-iron already in place. Next we build a low wall of bricks between 30 and 50 cm high. The floor of the night shelter should be built at this level and is best made of concrete or concrete tiles. In my opinion, this is the best floor for the night shelter. Of course it can also be made of fired and creosote-treated

wooden planks, particularly if there is a good chance you may need to move the aviary. The rest of the aviary, including the roof, is best made from tongue-and-groove pine board. In addition, you will need the following materials: wire mesh, wire thread and roof covering (such as tiles, slate, plastic corrugated sheets, fiberglass, etc.—there is a wide selection to choose from). Any planks that we use should be narrow; the narrower the better, since these are less subject to warping. Use the common aviary wire mesh which is six-sided; if we keep large parrot varieties then I prefer the square welded type wire mesh which is available in various thicknesses (1.25, 1.47 and 1.65 mm). It is best to use wired glass or safety glass. A gutter (maintenance-free aluminum is best) is very useful if not absolutely necessary.

We would also like to make some remarks about the shape and size of the aviary. If the size of a chicken or duck coop is usually determined by the number of chickens or ducks one plans to keep, with an aviary it is the other way around. We first determine the amount of space we have available, then determine the size of the aviary and finally the number of birds we can keep. And even then we must constantly beware of overpopulation. Of course an aviary can house a number of

If you have no ready-made location that meets these requirements, you will have to make the adjustments yourself by planting bushes, shrubs, flowers, trees, etc.

Another point to consider is that you do not build your aviary

birds, but if little squabbles are taking place on a regular basis, this is an indication that our aviary is overpopulated. Naturally, I have assumed that you have selected a compatible group of birds; not every bird can be placed with a given group! But no doubt you knew that already!

As far as the shape of the aviary is concerned, one last remark: keep the lines straight and simple. It is the contents of the aviary that should be the focus of attention, not the domes, steeples, towers, etc. You should also try to have the shape conform to the surroundings, both the ground plan and the aviary itself. As already said, the whole should fit in with the little piece of nature that you have created as smoothly as possible.

These budgerigars have access to indoor aviaries through large windows.

too low. The front height should be a minimum of 2 or 2½ meters if we are to achieve an esthetic result.

Most of the birds that we keep in the aviary can stay outdoors during the winter as well, providing they have good protection against wind and rain, and a draft-free night shelter for sleeping. A completely open section of the aviary is also quite essential—you might take note of how many birds are still in this part of the aviary in spite of, no, enjoying, a reasonably heavy shower. In this completely open section, then, the walls and top are all made of wire mesh. The floor is best made of sand, so that a natural effect can be brought about by planting several plants and shrubs, in which various bird species will build their nests. Grass, reeds and other low growth is necessary when we wish to house ground species, such as quail, etc., so that a natural floor—regularly turned over with a spade—with natural protection, offers these birds the kind of setting they might have in the wild. You might notice, too, how much they enjoy looking for insects when you are turning the ground over.

The covered portion of the aviary has a watertight roof (preferably made of a sheet of corrugated fiberglass or plastic, so that this part will still transmit

from mesh (and we are speaking here of the wall that adjoins the flight, of course). Personally, I am not in favor of this, because I feel it does not afford enough protection against the elements; and it also means that we cannot provide the birds with some heat in the night shelter, should this ever be desirable, since, with one wall made of mesh, that would now be senseless.

The floor of the covered section can also be of sand, and if we spray our plants regularly, we do not need to worry that these plants will not 'do' very well. Of course if you prefer to have a floor constructed of cement tiles, this is perfectly all right as well. Such a floor, however, should be

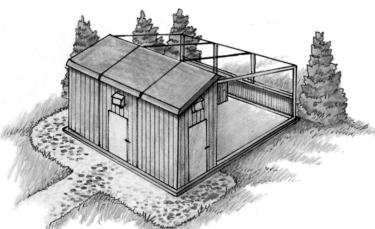

light), perhaps a back wall made of planking, although fiberglass would do just as well, and the rest is made of wire mesh. The dividing wall that can be built so that it is removable and separates the completely open area from the covered part of the flight (and which we might wish to put into place in extended periods of bad weather) is also made of mesh. Some fanciers even make the wall of the completely closed area

In this aviary each shelter has its own entrance.

generously covered with river sand, in which the birds really enjoy picking and sand bathing. With such a floor, the natural growth would consist of one or more lovely dead trees, supplemented with artificial perches, and live plants, placed in pots and tubs. Unfortunately, this does little to help create the natural effect that we are trying so hard to achieve.

The night shelter is a little more complicated. First of all, at the front of the aviary we build a little 'porch.' In order to sooner or later avoid the escape of birds, we will definitely have to work with this system. In this little porch, then, there are no birds. There are some five doors leading from it: 1) outer door; 2) door to covered section; 3) door to

quarantine station, punishment room for trouble makers, observation room, etc., while the other part is used for storing nesting boxes, perches, water and food containers, etc. The floors of both bottom halves can best be made of asbestos, concrete or tiles; the floor of the actual night shelter should also be made of concrete but covered with a layer of about 6 or 8 cm of river sand mixed with shell sand.

storage area; 4) door to the flight; 5) door to the night shelter.

Once in the little porch, of course, we close the door behind us to prevent the escape of any birds. Only then should we open the inner door leading to the flight. The next compartment is divided in half horizontally; the top half is the actual night shelter. The bottom half is split once more, this time vertically; one part is used for a mating room,

These outdoor aviaries will house several dozen pairs of doves.

The sides of the night shelter are made of safety glass; the division separating this part from the covered area could be made of wire if desired. The same applies to the inner aviary.

I would like to make a few more important comments on the building of the aviary before moving on to other types of bird

White-bellied Caique
(Pionites leucogaster)

staining or treating with carbolic acid all parts of the aviary—in fact, to help prevent the warping of the wood, you should treat all the wood with stain or carbolic acid before you even begin with the aviary! Even the wire should be given a coat of stain (use an almost dry brush) which also helps to make the birds a good deal more visible. The night shelter should not be painted, but it can be white-washed.

THE BIRD ROOM

This is really nothing more than an outside aviary made indoors, such as in an attic room, basement or other available room in the house. The 'building' of the bird room consists merely of fitting wire screens over the windows and building a little 'porch' to prevent the birds from escaping, by means of an extra wire door. The rest of the setup is the same as in an outside aviary. The bird room is used a great deal for breeding canaries and other birds that do not breed so readily in a (cold) outdoor aviary. A bird room is also very suitable for keeping the more exclusive species, particularly those birds that cannot take your local climate very well and do better in

housing. When pouring the foundation be sure to bury the wire mesh into the earth (about 20 cm) to deter rats and mice from entering the bird housing. It is also important to place wire in position when pouring the concrete to prevent it from cracking. The sides can be built using vertical tongue-and-groove boards. It speaks for itself that all windows, doors, etc. should be properly hung and should close tightly. To avoid puddles and the consequent rotting of materials, make sure the roof is built on a slant and extends on all sides. Naturally, the roof should be completely waterproof. The final touches consist of thoroughly

Designs for aviaries are limited only to your level of creativity.

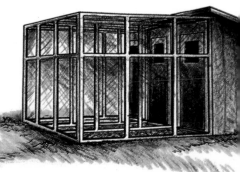

This indoor aviary for cockatiels, extends from floor to ceiling.

a climate-controlled aviary. Very expensive species, such as hummingbirds, honey and nectar birds, various tanagers and some parakeet species, are often kept in this type of bird housing. Bird rooms are often found among the more experienced fanciers. But the beginning bird enthusiast as well can achieve beautiful breeding results in a bird room. Yellow-bellied waxbills, red-eared waxbills, zebra finches and the like often breed more readily in such a bird room than in an aviary. Naturally we should try to achieve a natural effect; the floor consists of tiles upon which we

place a layer of beach sand, which of course we have to refresh regularly. We try to maintain as much natural shrubbery as possible, although of course these must be placed in tubs and pots. With a little artistic insight and imagination, we can create a beautiful piece of nature right inside our own home!

THE INDOOR AVIARY

These are used primarily for the keeping and breeding of tropical and sub-tropical birds. The indoor aviary can best be described as follows: it is a small aviary that we place in some room of the house or in an attic, around which we group a wealth of plants and in which we place a few adorable little singers or colorful birds. The setup is again the same as in an outside aviary.

Many people confuse an indoor aviary with a bird room. A bird room, however, is always an entire room set up as a bird room, not used for anything else by the inhabitants of the house; the indoor aviary is an aviary placed in a room. The indoor aviary is very popular of late;

The bird population seemed to be unconcerned by the fact that children played nearby on the floor.

We prefer not to delve into the details regarding cages, vitrines and other small types of bird housing, since these are very well known already. Vitrines are usually a closed type of bird housing with only the front and

"Treble breeder" cages with a small center compartment are useful when pairing one cock to two hens.

there are even a few manufacturers that make some ready-made models, and these certainly meet the necessary requirements. I have seen some indoor aviaries that were truly beautiful and in which, furthermore, successful breeding results were regularly achieved.

top made of wire. Through the use of an overabundant amount of shrubbery and effective lighting, a fairy tale effect can be achieved that is as enchanting as it is colorful. It is best to keep just a few couples, and if breeding boxes are made available, they will often come to breed. Cages, of course, are also commonly known. Yet we should keep a watchful eye on our choice here; the tall tower type cage, as an example, is generally not as suitable, and a lot of chrome cages do not meet the necessary requirements either. Keeping the following in mind should somewhat simplify your choice. See that a cage fits the dimensions of your bird. Give preference to a cage that comes with a few more doors, which makes cleaning and the like a lot easier. If you wish to achieve breeding results, you are well advised to use the so-called box cages. These are completely closed except for a wire bar front—horizontal bars for parakeet varieties and vertical bars for other bird species. It stands to reason that any kind of bird housing should be placed in a light location, though not in the full force of the sun and not in any kind of draft. These cages offer the most safety to a bird couple, which is why it is particularly in box cages that some very outstanding breeding results have come into existence, not even considering the annual successes booked with canaries, zebra finches, budgerigars and other commonly known bird species.

Horizontal bars are preferred for climbing.

FACILITIES AND MAINTENANCE

SITTING AND SLEEPING FACILITIES

We should use two kinds of perches for our birds. The first kind are the common, not too slender perches that have a somewhat flattened top; some can be attached in a stationary position while others can be affixed in a swinging position. They should be made of a hardwood. The swinging perches serve as playground toys; the stationary ones are 'resting benches,' which are also indispensable during the mating season. In aviaries that have lots of shrubbery, the various branches also serve as sitting and sleeping perches; some species, especially exotic birds, even build their nests in between the branches. Particularly during the

Perches should be made of hardwood and be available in varying dimensions.

summer, the birds make a lot of use of the bushes, yet it is still desirable to make separate sleeping facilities in the inner aviary and in the covered section; these should be round, stationary perches, placed in wind-free, draft-free locations. Another type of sleeping facility would be a few half-open nesting boxes, hung in the open section. We keep mentioning hardwood (stripped of its bark, of course) because it is most likely to remain lice-free. The perches should not be too thin, as our birds should not be able to completely encircle them with their toes; they should be able to completely relax on them. These perches will also help in deterring overgrown nails, especially if we ensure that the perches are not all the same thickness. This will help them in retaining supple leg muscles. Install your perches as high up as possible, because birds

Swinging perches provide amusement as well as perching accommodations.

instinctively like to sit as high up as they can. Don't be stingy with the perches; your birds should not have to fight for a sitting or sleeping place! Naturally, no perch should be hung underneath another one, since the droppings of the birds on the top might fall on the birds below. The same goes for hanging perches above any food, water or bathing dishes.

AVIARY GREENERY

In the covered section of the aviary we are pretty well forced to settle for some nicely formed dead trees. In the uncovered flight, however, we can place several small live trees and bushes, but they must be hardy growers and preferably be a hard leaf variety with a sturdy branch formation, or they will not be able to handle the struggle for existence. Not many plants can survive the daily confrontation with bird beaks!

All birds, such as the Perfect Lorikeet (Trichoglossus euteles), feel more secure in an environment that is well planted and natural in appearance.

Now you must not conclude that it is therefore better to substitute perches bought at the carpenter's for live plants. Live plants are absolutely essential, not only because many birds build their nests in the branches, or sleep in them during the evening and night, but also because they give the aviary an attractive appearance. We must also not forget that many shrubs and plants lure countless insects, of which the birds make grateful use, particularly during the breeding period. Finally, the greenery offers protection to the birds whenever they are alarmed. As you can see, there are several points in favor of live greenery.

However, it is not always easy to provide good care for the plants, especially not when the aviary is inhabited by budgerigars and canaries. Still, I strongly recommend you use live plants, perhaps replacing any dead ones once a year. These do not need to be expensive species; buying some shrubs that do not perhaps have exactly the proper shape— and are therefore cheaper—will fill our needs perfectly. Let's divide the greenery into three categories:

I. A few trees that offer good nesting places:
Silver fir *(Abies alba)*; Nordmann fir *(Abies nordmanniana)*; Scotch pine *(Pinus silvestris)*; Austrian pine *(Pinus nigra)*; Douglas fir *(Pseudotsuga taxifolia)*; spruce fir *(Picea excelsa)*; European larch *(Laris decidua)*; northern white cedar *(Thuja occidentalis)*; oriental or Chinese cedar *(Thuja orientalis)*; English holly *(Ilex aguifolium)*; common boxwood

(Buxus sempervirens); common privet (Ligustrum vulgare); false spirea (Sorbaria sorbifolia); Japanese spirea (Spiraea japonica); snowberry (Symphoricarpo albus); common juniper (Juniperus communis); and English ivy (Hedera helix).

II. A few species that are known to be sturdy growers, and some of which offer excellent breeding places as well, particularly when they are artfully pruned:

climber (Rosa multiflora); European hornbeam (Carpinus betulus); and pretty well any Prunus species, mock orange, Viburnum species, sea buckthorn and several Cotoneaster species.

III. Ground Cover:
Grass sods are a welcome choice. If the grass is regularly kept moist, we will often be able to see the birds romping in it. I need not tell you that this is an inspiring

Various nonpoisonous trees and shrubs can be planted in the aviary.

European elderberry (Sambucus nigra); common elderberry (Sambucus canadensis); Oregon holly grape (Mahonia aquifolius); rhododendron (Rhododendron ponticum); English hawthorn (Crataegus monigyna); 'New Dawn'

and often comical sight! Grass sods are also perfectly suitable for planting in an aviary that houses just exotic birds, though parakeet varieties are of course the ones that put on the show of frolicking in the grass. It is a good idea to maintain a little lawn in any kind of aviary, because many birds like to search for insects in the grass or to lie in it and enjoy a little sunbathing. In addition, little

21

Chinese painted quail and other ground birds enjoy building a nest in grass that has become somewhat overgrown.

It is also wise to plant some reeds and maize in one or more corners of the aviary, as this will do much to keep short the nails of many tropical species (such as the nutmeg finch and the white-headed mannikin), while a few rough stones (such as flagstones) will also serve as little 'nail clippers' for our birds. Most nurseries provide brief care instructions with the plants that we buy. As an alternative, we can always write down the names of any plants we buy and look up their proper care in a plant book in the library. We could hardly go into details in this book regarding the care of all the plants mentioned. Besides, there is ample literature available on this subject.

A hollowed tree trunk may be preferred by some species.

BREEDING POSSIBILITIES

The first requirement is that the nesting boxes exceed the number of mated pairs. It may sound strange, but only when the birds have a more than ample choice of nesting areas will they actually come to breed. Although the type and size of nesting boxes required by the various species are often mentioned as part of our individual species descriptions, I feel a few general remarks are apropos here. For one thing, you cannot assume that the type of nesting boxes prescribed in those descriptions will necessarily always be used. Experience has shown that a breeder in an enclosed nest may just decide to make an open nest or make use of a half-open nesting box. The so-called half breeders, in half enclosed nests in particular, such as the well-known zebra finch, may choose half a coconut (an open nest), a whole coconut (an enclosed nest) or a half open nesting box to start a family, even though there are

Provide various types of nesting containers from which the birds can choose.

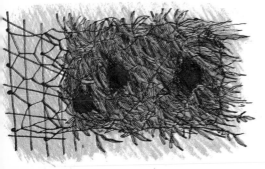

plenty of choices available. And don't be surprised if all of these choices take place in the same season, as has happened to me on more than one occasion! As you can see, the breeding process may hold some surprises for you. In any event, be sure to provide plenty of nesting facilities for your birds—preferably at least twice as many as there are breeding couples.

There are two kinds of breeding facilities:

1) the natural variety and
2) the artificial kind.

1) The Natural Variety

When selecting the greenery for our aviary, we should make sure that each piece has several fork-shaped branch formations that are ideal locations for nest

Above: *Red and Green Macaws (Ara chloroptera).*
Below: *Although functional, some nesting containers may prove impractical for nest checks.*

White-headed Munia (Lonchura maja) and other small birds may prefer to nest in wicker baskets.

building. If there are not enough of these forks present, or none at all, we can solve this problem in a few years by doing some extensive pruning. It is faster, however, to use wire to bind a few branches together to form a good nesting place. Some ground breeders also like to make their nests in clumps of reeds, rushes, heather bushes and the like. If your aviary is large enough, you should include these plants as well.

2) The Artificial Kind

I am sure that these are sufficiently well known, so that I will merely enumerate the various models:

a) nesting boxes—*i.e.* open, half open, closed and as a block (birch blocks and beechwood blocks, as examples).

b) nesting boxes and 'hives'—coconuts, baskets, nestpans, etc.

c) various—such as corkbark, bunch of heather, bunch of straw, etc.

Perhaps it is superfluous to mention this, but I would like to point out that we should not make these nesting facilities available to the birds until early spring. All artificial nesting materials should be taken out of the aviary after the breeding season, at which time we can thoroughly clean it.

During the winter we have the opportunity to again stain or apply carbolic acid to everything inside and out, and in this way disinfect it.

We should keep in mind that aviary birds in top notch health only grow from baby birds in top notch health and that it is particularly the nesting facilities and nests themselves that shelter many disease-producing bacteria and germs.

*Bengalese Society Finches (*Lonchura maja*) prefer open baskets which the male will fill with anything soft and weavable.*

MAINTENANCE OF THE AVIARY

Let's assume that we are starting out with a new aviary, built in accordance with the specifications given. There are, therefore, a minimum number of corners and angles, and we have done a thorough job with staining or applying carbolic acid. The floor is either made of natural soil or covered with pure river or sharp sand.

1) The first order of business, then, is maintenance of the ground. The sand on the floors must be replaced and the earth must be turned over and dug up with a spade. The frequency of this operation depends on the size of the aviary and the number of its inhabitants. I cannot, therefore, give you specific

rules, but I suggest you stick to the following guideline: never have a dirty floor; it is better to have worked too hard than not enough.

2) At least once a year in the spring all perches, nesting boxes, etc. should be thoroughly cleaned and

twigs, etc. be removed. The entire structure should be thoroughly hosed off. Replace any dead plants, if possible.

3) Concerning the aviary as a whole, it is advisable to place our birds in flight cages in the spring for just a short time to give us the opportunity to

Each year the aviary must be completely disinfected.

disinfected. The shrubs, which are Nature's perches for our birds, should be pruned and any dead or rotting branches,

really do a good job in cleaning both the interior and exterior of the aviary, repair leaks, fill in cracks, mend any holes in the wire, check the gutter, check locks and hinges, etc. In short, bring the entire aviary back

Proper maintenance will secure a healthy environment.

into top form! If we check and repair the aviary every year, we will not likely get a lot of surprises at once, especially during the busy season.

4) Maintenance of the nesting facilities has already been discussed; the same applies, however, to feeding dishes, drinking fountains, bathing dishes, etc. Whenever we give water to our birds, which takes place at least once a day, we can clean the dishes and fountains at that time.

Universal food, bread soaked in water, chick rearing food, etc. should also be replaced daily, and the dishes these foods are served on should then be thoroughly cleaned. If you have automatic water hoppers, these can be cleaned once a week; the same applies to automatic seed hoppers.

Everything must be kept spotlessly clean throughout the year, but in the spring (and also in the fall if your birds are spending the winter outdoors as well), everything should be given a thorough cleaning, including disinfection and necessary repairs.

BIRD SPECIES AND THEIR CARE

FINCHES

With his scarlet coloring above, the male VIRGINIAN CARDINAL (*Richmondena cardinalis*) certainly makes a striking appearance in any aviary. During the mating season the feathers even lose their grayish seams, really doing justice to the beautiful cardinal's robe.

The hen is considerably duller in coloring, so that distinguishing between the sexes and obtaining a true pair does not pose any problems. I would point out that the much less vivid coloring of the hen, particularly above, is necessary for protecting her during breeding. It is quite a job for enemies to spot her! The Virginian cardinal hails from the eastern United States, over Mexico, to Belize. The birds are becoming more and more park and garden birds, particularly the somewhat smaller form from Florida. They are rarely found high up in the trees. They spend more and more of their time near people, seeking their food in orchards, city parks and gardens. Both during the spring and summer they form pairs, while later in the year they can be seen in family groups (parents and their young); during severe winters they form fairly large groups and remain around built-up communities looking for food. Around March they disappear again in pairs to go to their breeding places. In spite of their frequent close vicinity to man, they are very cautious and timid; during the breeding period they are quite aggressive. This is why we should only keep this species together with larger birds. The aviary housing them should be

The Virginian Cardinal (*Richmondena cardinalis*) *can live for more than 20 years in captivity.*

located in a peaceful setting, so that we can improve our chances for achieving breeding results. We can then enjoy—from a distance—their strong, full and melodious song that is so full of variety. Even during clear moonlit nights the male will give voice to his repertoire. Cardinals like to build their nests in thorny bushes and also in very thick shrubbery.

Both sexes work at building the nest, and work they do, completing their home in about four days. We provide them with such nesting materials such as small roots, stalks, blades of grass, small twigs, moss and dry leaves. They line the inside of their nest with soft small blades of grass. The female lays four or five eggs that vary greatly in color; they can be almost white, greenish, bluish, blue-green, yellowish or brown-red in background, with very regularly spaced spots and blotches, again varying in color, among others red, yellow, gray, brown, orange and violet. In the wild, particularly when weather conditions are favorable and food is plentiful, they will generally have two clutches per season, but in the aviary we can be very grateful if they will have one brood in the spring or summer. Only the hen sits on the eggs—usually a good fourteen days. Fifteen days after coming out of the eggs the young leave the nest, but they continue to be fed at least another twelve days by both parents before they are totally independent and seek food by themselves. During those twelve days the parents feed their young mainly larvae, insect eggs, ant eggs and cherries; during the last few days they also feed them berries and buckwheat seeds. In addition, we should not forget the following seeds: oats, panicum millet, sunflower seeds and canary seed. Universal food, mealworms and enchytrae, rusks, greens, grated or dried cheese, and apple are also welcome and can be offered on a varying basis year in and year out. As far as greens are concerned, I would add that the sprouting (spilled) seeds in the aviary, lettuce and little twigs with fresh green buds are very good for the birds, and these are a good means to avoid their becoming overweight. As we mentioned in the first general section, we must never offer too many mealworms—just two or three per bird per day. If we have more than one pair of cardinals in an aviary, we will need to separate them during the breeding period to avoid fighting and to promote a steady forming of pairs. Nesting boxes are not generally needed here, but we will have to make sure that there are some thick needle-type trees

(small ones) and frequently pruned leaf-bearing trees. The hen will rarely use a flat nest. During the breeding cycle, the hen will be fed by the cock, but both parents feed the young; finely chopped red meat, hard-boiled egg and dried grated cheese are three favorites of the

The Green Cardinal (Gubernatrix cristata) is from Argentina.

young birds. The young will need to be removed from the cage before the start of the next breeding cycle. It is pleasant to report that cardinals in captivity can sometimes reach an age of twenty years or even more.

The GREEN CARDINAL (Gubernatrix cristata) comes from Argentina and can certainly be

Unlike the previous cardinal species, the male Red Crested takes turns with the female incubating their eggs.

usually sits and sings in the immediate vicinity, which, incidentally, he does pretty well! The hen also hatches the three to four eggs by herself, which takes about twelve days. At that time the cock will also go into action. We offer egg-food, mealworms and a large variety of insects and direct replacements of these. If we stick to the menu that we outlined for the Virginian cardinal the birds should live in good health for many years. Both the Virginian and green cardinals can spend the winter outdoors, though I personally think the latter species is better brought into an unheated area indoors for that season.

The well-known RED CRESTED CARDINAL *(Paroaria coronata)* comes from southern Brazil, Argentina and Bolivia, and makes an attractive appearance with its white and red coloring. If they are housed in a reasonably well-protected aviary, they can spend the winter outdoors. They are quite pleasant as cage birds as well, but if we would like to breed them then a roomy aviary is, of course, the appropriate housing for them. They prefer to build their nest in dense bushes, putting it together with twigs, blades of grass and leaf veins, and lining the interior with horsehair. They just naturally like to be 'higher up,' so that low aviaries do not suit them very well. Their nest is usually built at two to four meters from the ground. Their clutch consists of three or four eggs which are spotted in gray at the blunt end. Although individual birds are peaceful, a couple might cause a little trouble with other birds during the breeding period, but since the previously discussed

kept by beginning fanciers. Although they are considerably less aggressive than the other cardinal species, they can take care of themselves sufficiently well during the breeding period, so that they can still be kept together with the Virginian cardinal. The nest is usually built in a half-open nesting box or even in a bush (cup-shaped). For nesting material they use grass, small twigs, separated sisal string, etc. The hen does most of the building herself; the cock cardinal species can also take care of themselves, it should not be any great problem. When breeding in an aviary, the birds make grateful use of any woven nest baskets, or half-open nesting boxes, hung at least 1 1/2 meters from the ground. For extra building materials we can supply them with heather stalks. Cock and hen take turns sitting on the eggs; the hatching period is twelve to fourteen days. Once the young are out of the egg, both parents will feed them. After fourteen days, the fledglings leave the nest but will continue to be fed by the cock for at least another two weeks. The breeding period takes place from April into the fall, but if we are not careful they will continue to breed during the winter, even with severe frost, so that we must either remove the nesting facilities or separate the couple for the winter. For feeding requirements we refer you to the previous cardinal species.

The BLACK-TAILED HAWFINCH (*Coccothraustes migratoria*) hails from northeastern China. There they live in woods of leaf-bearing trees and build their nests on thin twigs far away from the tree trunk, at about one to two meters from the ground. Because of their sturdy build we can keep them together with the species previously discussed (we already have a colorful collection here!). They breed well and regularly; for nesting material we can supply them with blades of grass, thin twigs, dried grass and some wet earth and spider webs with which they hold the nest together. The clutch consists of three to five eggs, the color of which is bright gray to light green-gray with gray and dark brown circles, spots and stripes. The female hatches the eggs by herself. The breeding season takes place during the months of May and June. At that time the female is fed by the cock. After eleven days the young come out of the eggs and spend some twelve days in the nest, during which time the cock will feed them. The young will be independent after about twenty

*Black-tailed Hawfinch
(Coccothraustes migratoria)*

days. For food requirements please refer to the previously mentioned species. Both the male and female sing very well, though the female's voice is softer in tone and timbre. This species is quite tolerant by nature and can be kept together with other birds.

When kept in the company of smaller birds, the BRAZILIAN BLUE GROSBEAK (Cyanocompsa cyanea) is certainly a very pleasant little friend. They originate from eastern and southern Brazil where they can often be seen in the fields and at the edge of the woods; they are seen considerably less frequently in small woods and very rarely indeed in the high trees of the jungles. This explains why they are quite easily caught, even though they usually live alone or in pairs. Only during the winter do they form small groups.

These birds are excellent singers. It is a shame, however, that the beautiful dark blue plumage with black and purple-green reflections becomes discolored in so many specimens when kept in captivity, even though they are fed a wealth of insects. I would advise keeping this bird only as an aviary bird, as my experience has been that they are less suitable as cage birds. The semicircle-shaped nest is usually built in fairly dense bushes from blades of grass, leaf-veins and the like. They use moss, fine sawdust or decayed wood dust to line the nest. The clutch usually consists of four eggs that are hatched only by the hen (thirteen days hatching period). Initially the breeding period will fall in June, perhaps even the beginning of July, but after we have these birds in the aviary for a few years, they tend to start the breeding period progressively later and later in the year. As long as the weather is favorable we need not concern ourselves with this. The young leave the nest after only ten days but continue to be fed by both parents for quite some time. During the breeding period, in particular, we can enjoy the exuberant singing of the male.

The LIGHT BLUE GROSBEAK (Cyanocompsa parellina) is also an excellent singer. This species hails from eastern and southern Mexico and is regularly shipped to Europe, to be sold for reasonable prices. This species has been occupying European aviaries since 1895. Their care

*The Owl Finch (*Poephila bichenovii*) comes from northwestern Australia and the Northern Territory.*

parallels that required by the Brazilian blue grosbeak.

I would now like to let several colorful birds pass in review. These are better not kept with the cardinal species, since this may well lead to problems. Since these birds are very colorful, it is advisable to treat them with extra care. You may be aware of the fact that the linnet, when kept in captivity, has difficulty in retaining already mentioned. Be sure to give them pine and spruce twigs with plenty of bark on them—they will pick at these with lots of enthusiasm, and it will be very beneficial for their red coloring. Some bird keepers recommend serving hard-boiled eggs and milk powder as strength foods during the molt. There are also good color foods available on the market today, and although they

Evening Grosbeak

the red in its plumage after the molt; this is also the case with several tropical and sub-tropical birds (you might bring to mind the Virginian cardinal!). In the first place we must pay ample attention to the aviary, to see that it is very airy and light. Then we must be aware of the fact that, in the wild, color finches eat a great many insects; next to seed; in fact, we should provide them with universal food, ant eggs, buds from young twigs, etc. throughout the year, while a good variety of seed mix should also be present, though it usually is not touched if there are plenty of other foods are meant for canaries, they should not be forgotten for our color finches either! Color finches are very peace loving in community aviaries, and if there is ample dense greenery, they will repeatedly breed well.

I would like to introduce the INDIGO BUNTING *(Passerina cyanea)* as the first color finch. This species comes from eastern North America, Canada and Mexico, as well as Central America to Panama, Cuba and

The bright coloring belongs to the male Indigo Bunting.

the Bahamas. They breed only in eastern Canada and northeastern America, from mid-April to mid-May. At the end of September they migrate to the south, sometimes in very large flocks which stay together in their winter abodes; they are usually only in pairs in their breeding locations, where they live a somewhat timid and withdrawn existence. In the aviary they enjoy sitting in low shrubs and on the ground. They sing often and long, though their song is comparatively simple and monotonous. The birds make a semi-ball-shaped nest, about one meter from the ground, in dense bushes. The hen builds the nest by herself, although the cock will bring her nesting material in the form of stalks, leaf veins, leaf fibers, wool and cotton thread, even pieces of paper and spider webs. The inside of the nest is lined with fine little roots, horsehair and thin blades of grass and leaves; everything is beautifully woven and finished. The clutch consists of four or five bluish or light green-white eggs. The hen hatches the eggs by herself, while the cock will feed her on the nest and guard the maternity ward! Usually this species has but one clutch per year. The hatching period takes about thirteen days. The young leave the nest after eleven days but continue to be fed for quite some time by the parents before they are independent. They are kept a great deal in cages and aviaries in their native tropical countries too—perhaps one of the reasons why their export has become so difficult. When the birds are given a somewhat private, roomy aviary, breeding results are not an exception; crossbreeding has been successful a few times with canaries and nonpareil buntings.

This brings us to the beautiful *Passerina ciris*. The natural habitat of this bird is the southern part of the United States, Mexico, Central America to Panama, Cuba and the Bahamas. The northern areas mentioned are the breeding locations. They are not very timid, which might account for the success booked in the breeding

department! This bird will sing at night too, just like the nightingale, and can also sing while flying upwards, just like the skylark! The nest is constructed close to the ground in hedges and blackberry bushes, and is made of grass, fine little roots, hair and spider webs. The eggs are light blue in color, with white and purple-to-red spots and stripes. They are very good aviary birds that will gladly rear the young of other birds too! With the proper care they can attain a ripe old age; I have known cases of birds that lived ten, thirteen and sixteen years respectively in good health in an aviary with plenty of dense greenery. The hatching period is thirteen days; after eleven days the young leave the nest. The hen builds the nest and hatches the young by herself, and often even with the rearing of the young the cock does not so much as extend

*The bright coloration of the male Painted Bunting (*Passerina ciris*) fade in captivity.*

a hand (by way of speaking!); he will sit in close proximity to the nest, singing quietly and clearly. The care required by this species parallels that of the previous species.

The VARIED BUNTING (Passerina versicolor) comes from southern Arizona, northern and southern Texas, and Mexico. The cock sings quite well and will give voice to his repertoire during the morning and evening hours, but not during the day. The breeding usually starts early in May. They prefer to use open baskets and 'hives' in low dense shrubs. For building materials they prefer to use plant fibers and

The male Rainbow Bunting. The female is very dull by comparison.

pieces of wool. The hen builds the nest by herself; she usually lays just two green-brown, violet-brown spotted eggs which are hatched in about thirteen days.

The RAINBOW BUNTING (Passerina leclancheri) lives in southwestern Mexico. The female normally lays two eggs that are bluish green in color and have a purplish marking. The birds give preference to open nesting baskets and canary boxes that are to be hung in dense cedar bushes and similar shrubs. For building materials we should provide wool, grass, coconut fibers, leaf veins and the like. The breeding period falls in May through July. They usually rear two clutches per year, particularly if they have access to a rich variety of animal food.

The LAZULI BUNTING (Passerina amoena) comes from British Columbia and the western part of America. The birds migrate to the south for the winter, spending it in Mexico (where they are caught for export) and in the southern United States. During the migration the cocks will fly ahead of the hens in large groups. In the aviary they are very lively birds, always active, and very entertaining as well with their fairly inquisitive ways. Their nest is semi-ball-shaped and is constructed in dense shrubbery about one meter from the ground. Breeding successes in the aviary are still only booked on a sporadic basis. Nevertheless it is a pleasant bird to keep in a community aviary, no doubt also due to its peace-loving nature.

Another active little bird is the OLIVE FINCH (Euethia olivacea) from Cuba, Jamaica and Haiti. The natives consider this species to be a bit of a pest because the birds damage their sugar cane crops by drawing the marrow from the drying sugar cane. These little birds also like to steal honey from beehives! It follows that if we are to keep these sweet tooths really satisfied, we will have to offer them a piece of honeycomb regularly! This species is sometimes known as *Tiaris olivacea*. For nesting material they use dried parts of plants, fine roots, hair, little feathers and fruit fuzz. The female lays two or three blue-white eggs with brown or black-brown dots which often form pretty little circles. The breeding period takes place in the spring, although some clutches are bred later in the year. It is possible to crossbreed them with the Cuban finch.

The well-known, sometimes quite aggressive CUBAN FINCH *(Tiaris canora)* is also seen in Florida on occasion (as a wanderer), although his country of origin, as the name implies, is Cuba. When kept as a pair they are peaceful aviary birds; if the cock is kept without a mate, however, he can be a regular little terrorist towards the other aviary inhabitants. As a couple, though, they are excellent. It is rather strange that it sometimes happens, particularly in the wild, that either the cock or the hen suddenly decides to pull their own nest apart, desert the eggs or throw certain young out of the nest. This does not mean that this couple is unsuitable for breeding; we can look forward to a good brood of perhaps four or five young if the weather is good the next season. It also happens that the parents throw out just the young cocks or just the young hens and continue rearing those left in the nest as if nothing ever happened (natural sex limitation).

For building materials they use coconut and agave fibers, sisal and hemp string (separated), hair, small feathers and grass. They frequently re-use an old nest. The hen alone hatches the eggs (eleven to thirteen days), but the young are fed by both parents. After twelve days, sometimes not until seventeen days, the young leave the nest; but the cock will

The Cuban Finch has a deep black face framed with a broad circular band of bright yellow.

continue to feed them, now on his own, sometimes for more than a month. The hen generally begins a new brood. The care required parallels that indicated for the previous species; in other words, they must have universal food, strength food, ant eggs, hard-boiled egg, insects, mealworms, leaf lice (to be found on the elder tree and on roses), little spiders,

Diuca Finch (Diuca diuca)*, the male possesses the blue-gray coloration.*

greens (chickweed) and the like in addition, of course, to a good mix of tropical seed varieties.

A beautiful bird, often thought by ornithologists to be the transitional form between cardinals and real crown finches,

is the fairly expensive, but nevertheless gorgeous CRIMSON FINCH *(Rhodospingus cruentus)* from Peru and Ecuador. These birds breed in open 'hives' and in half open nesting boxes. They will also use the old nests left by weavers. The hen hatches by herself and builds the nest by herself too. Both feed the young. The clutch consists of three or four blue-white eggs. The hatching period is eleven to twelve days. The young leave the nest after ten to fourteen days. In the aviary these birds are very tolerant by nature, although this might be less true during the breeding period, but serious irregularities are unlikely to occur.

The primarily blue-gray DIUCA FINCH *(Diuca diuca)* from Chile is another lovely bird that beginners should not have too much trouble keeping. This finch sings quite nicely, is an everything-eater and will breed regularly even in a smaller aviary. Their roughly constructed nest is made in dense bushes about two meters from the ground; they will also use nesting boxes. If they are given some insect food and their aviary has a fairly peaceful location, breeding results will certainly not be long off.

The AMERICAN GOLDFINCH *(Carduelis tristis)* comes from western Canada and the western regions of the United States, but it is even seen along the Gulf of Mexico during the winter. The clutch consists of three to five vivid green-white eggs, which the hen hatches by herself (fourteen days). These birds can be crossbred with canaries, and if we serve them the menu outlined for canaries, we should be able to enjoy them in good health for a considerable period of time.

A better known bird is the HOODED SISKIN *(Carduelis cucullatus)* from Venezuela, Trinidad, Cuba and Puerto Rico. Thanks to this bird, we now have 'red' canaries. When this species is housed in a roomy aviary, they will breed quite readily. The clutch consists of three or four bluish white eggs that have red-brown markings; the hen hatches them by herself. She also rears the

As the name implies, the nicely voiced GRAY SINGING FINCH *(Serinus leucopygia)* is primarily gray. He comes from north Africa south to the equator. The clutch usually consists of three or four white or very light green eggs with black markings, and is deposited in an artfully woven nest built high in a small tree or bush. At first glance the nest looks a little like that of the

*The beautiful song of the Gray Singing Finch (*Serinus leucopygia*) makes up for its unimpressive coloration.*

young birds by herself, but once they have flown out, the cock takes care of them. The care required for the hooded siskin is the same as that required by the canary.

canary. For building materials we supply them with all kinds of little roots, fibers, hay and grass. The interior is lined with little feathers and hair. The hen builds the nest by herself. The breeding period takes place from May through most of August, sometimes even to the beginning of September. When feeding and housing are up

The Saffron Finch incubates for 12 to 13 days.

to snuff, a couple may have three to four broods per season. The hatching period is about two weeks. After about two or three weeks the young leave the nest but continue to be fed by both parents for quite some time; in fact, the cock will even continue feeding them for a few days after the hen has started a new cycle. The gray singing finch is often crossed with canaries. Be sure that your birds are never subjected to drafts, and offer them insects as frequently as you can. Add a disinfectant to their drinking water, as they are often bothered by infected eyes; recently imported birds in particular seem to suffer from this ailment. Some diluted boric acid lotion can do wonders!

The YELLOW-RUMPED SERIN *(Serinus atrogularis)* lives in South Africa to deep into the Congo. Their clutch consists of three bright blue eggs with red-brown markings. For other particulars please refer to the gray singing finch. The yellow-rumped serin is kept quite a lot both as an aviary and cage bird; while its singing abilities are quite good, they do not match those of its cousin, the gray singing finch.

The SAFFRON FINCH *(Sicalis flaveola)* can be found in the wilds of Peru, Ecuador, Colombia, Venezuela and into the Guianas. These birds usually build their nest in a tree hollow, which is why we should supply them with the closed type nesting boxes in the aviary. Their clutch consists of three or four white eggs with just a few sparse black or gray markings. It is not unusual for them to have a few squabbles with other birds during the breeding time, and they may well inspect the nests of these birds too! This is why we should keep just one couple in an aviary, along with some of the sturdier finch species that can take care of themselves. If we wish the birds to breed, it will be absolutely necessary to supply them with a great many insects. Greens must not be forgotten either.

The BLACKHEADED SISKIN *(Carduelis magellanicus)* requires an aviary that has a great deal of dense vegetation. It can be kept together with a few larger birds and needs a lot of variety in insects as extra food. They build their nest quite close to the ground and make it from stalks, fibers and blades of grass; the interior is lined with fruit fuzz. The clutch consists of three to five bright blue eggs with red-brown markings, which are hatched by the female (thirteen days). This species is also suitable as a cage bird. It is often crossed with the canary.

The alario finches, with their typical deeply indented tail and their lightly hooked beak, make excellent aviary birds. The most important representative is the ALARIO FINCH *(Serinus alario)* from South Africa. The primarily brown-red female lays two or three, sometimes five, dull blue eggs that have reddish brown markings. Their nest is built close to the ground, is cup-shaped and is constructed of grass, wool and, occasionally, little feathers. In the aviary they will often use half-open nesting boxes, but I would recommend that you plan to have dense vegetation, since they enjoy building a free-standing nest. A large variety of seeds needs to be supplied to them if

Alario Finch

they are to be coaxed to breed. Because of their close relationship to the canary, and because they have a pleasant song, they are sometimes crossed with the canary. I personally do not feel that the song is improved by this.

The well-known ARABIAN GOLDEN SPARROW *(Passer euchlorus)* hails from southern Arabia and the Abyssinian coast. The hen lays two or three light brown or white eggs that have gray or green-yellow markings. The eggs are often covered with a greenish haze. Their large, quite roughly constructed nest is made of grass and twigs and is generally well hidden in thick shrubbery.

The GOLDEN SPARROW *(Passer luteus)* comes from northeastern Africa and central Africa. The hen lays three or four green-white eggs with gray and brown markings, which she deposits into a cup-formed nest. The nest itself is made of grass and little twigs. These charming and lovely birds like cozy,

Blackheaded Siskin
*(*Carduelis magellanicus*)*

community style living, also evidenced by their community breeding in colonies. I have seen groups of hundreds of nests close together in just a few trees during my study tour in Africa. In the aviary they prefer to build their nests in thick bushes, although they will also use nesting boxes. The nesting boxes should not be hung higher than two meters. The breeding period takes place between May and November. The birds usually have two or three broods in a season. The hen hatches the eggs by herself, and the hatching period is ten days. After two weeks, sometimes sooner, the young leave the nest. Crossbreeding has taken place on various occasions with the common sparrow, although, of course, it is never a simple matter to bring about such a cross. Due to their pleasant song, their lively nature and their tolerance even during the breeding period, these birds are very popular among the fanciers, as is the previous species.

This completes the first collection of birds that can all be kept together in an aviary and require a good assortment of seeds, in addition to insects and universal food; they do not make any further demands of the bird keeper.

WEAVERS

One of the many things that set weavers (Ploceidae) apart from the real finches (Fringillidae) which we have just covered is the different style of nest building. In addition, weavers have ten flight feathers in their wings. The species live primarily in Africa, Indonesia, Australia and Madagascar. At the moment there are several ornithologists that prefer to classify some of these species under the so-called grass finches; this is a change that should only be applauded. Nevertheless, we shall not concern ourselves with this change in the nomenclature (really an improvement from many points of view), but I refer you to *The Complete Birds of the World* by Michael Walters (T.F.H. Publications, Inc.) in which this subject is extensively covered. In the meantime, we will stay with the old classification, which also has its advocates, and will not tire the reader with biological technicalities which are rarely of interest to the layman.

I would like to start by introducing a few true weavers; this group has some 160

The male Golden Sparrow (Passer luteus).

members, but only a few are known among the fanciers because many require large aviaries, and they can be quite restless by nature. Distinguishing between the sexes is also very

Experience has taught me that they will breed quite readily, providing they are not disturbed. The hen lays four or five very light green-blue eggs. The hatching period is thirteen days, and the

difficult. Even the display of the cock does not positively identify the bird to be a cock because some females have exactly the same tendency. Quite a number of broods in captivity are deserted because the birds are very timid and often lay unfertilized eggs. Their menu cannot be called complete unless they have constant access to live insects. If we can meet all these demands, then the MADAGASCAR WEAVER *(Foudia madagascariensis)* from Madagascar, Mauritius and St. Helena is a good choice.

Smith's Golden Weaver
(Ploceus subaureus aureoflavus)

hen hatches the eggs by herself. The cock will bring food once the young have crawled out of the egg. Incidentally strangely enough, this weaver is not a colony breeder, which is the case with the following bird.

The SPOTTED-BACKED WEAVER *(Malimbus, Ploceus,* or *Hyphantornis cucullatus)* is from the western regions of Africa. Just like the previous species, the spotted-backed weaver is an excellent choice for the beginning fancier. It cannot be kept together with small birds, however, and we should not keep more than one couple together either, to prevent fights that could quite possibly continue to the death. Time and again we will be fascinated by the change in the cock's plumage after the breeding period; he will assume the plumage of his

The male Paradise Whydah's two central feathers are present only during the breeding season.

spouse, so that you will not be able to tell them apart. This is quite a change from the marriage clothing he wears during the breeding period! All in all, these birds are only very moderate breeders in an aviary; in spite of their many artfully woven nests, which will continue to intrigue us, they rarely rear a good clutch.

The whydahs that I would now like to introduce to you are all so-called nesting parasites; that is to say that they deposit their eggs in the nests of other birds and have nothing further to do with their clutch. This is why it is extremely difficult to achieve breeding results in an aviary, as you can imagine. The well-known PARADISE WHYDAH *(Steganura paradisea)* lays her eggs in the nest of the fire finch, so that these birds should be housed in a large aviary if we wish to improve our chances of achieving breeding results. Various varieties of the paradise whydah are found in the eastern part of Africa. The QUEEN WHYDAH or SHAFT-TAILED WHYDAH *(Tetraenura regia)* from South Africa deposits her eggs in the nests of blue pheasants, and other species belonging to the *Estrilda* genus. Both species require a good brand of tropical seed, many insects and direct replacements of these, and fresh bathing water daily. The PINTAILED WHYDAH *(Vidua serena* or *Vidua macroura)* lays her eggs in the nests of the St. Helena waxbill and very likely also in those of the red-eared waxbill and other waxbill species. It may be of interest to note that in the wild this whydah has some ten to fifty hens! They live south of the Sahara. Another lovely bird is the GIANT WHYDAH *(Diatropura progne)* from Africa, who also surrounds himself with quite a harem of perhaps as many as fifty hens and can best, no doubt, be kept in an aviary along with some feminine beauties! It seems best to house the birds in the aviary before they have changed to their breeding plumage; in this way the gradual

eggs in the nests of the St. Helena waxbill, the firefinches and, in the aviary, even in those of zebra finches.

The WAXBILLS consist of many species in Africa plus species in Indonesia and Australia among others. Outside of the breeding period, it is virtually impossible to

change from their 'resting suit' to their 'groom's suit' will not alarm the other birds. Unlike the giant whydah with his long tail, the SENEGAL COMBASSOU (Vidua chalybeata) from northwestern Africa has a tail that is of normal proportions. This bird lays its

Male Queen Whydahs in full dress with their 25 cm long tails.

distinguish between the sexes. The eggs are usually white, are hatched in about eleven to thirteen days, and the young leave the nest after eleven to sixteen

Firefinch
(*Lagonostica senegala*)

days. Waxbills are more peaceful and quiet than the true weaver group, but a lot of species are also very timid, which causes many a clutch to fail. Consequently, peace and quiet is a primary requirement for an aviary housing these birds. I would like to add a practical piece of advice, namely, that you keep one or two hens in reserve; you see, it often happens that a certain couple will not breed or that their clutches keep failing to survive. However, when such a couple is split, everything often goes without a hitch. It is also often said of these birds that they can be easily used to hatch the eggs or rear the young of other birds; my experience, however, has been that this can virtually be done only by the well-known Bengalese and, less frequently, by zebra finches.

The FIREFINCH, which you may have guessed is primarily red in coloring, will breed quite readily in the aviary, especially if there are some secluded little spots for them to use. This bird, which is scientifically known as *Lagonostica senegala*, comes from West Africa. Their nest is built by both the cock and the hen and is made of hair, leaves, wool, sisal and blades of grass. It is quite roughly constructed and bullet-shaped. They will also use nesting boxes, old weaver nests, etc. Birds not kept in captivity will even build a nest under the eaves. In an indoor aviary they will also breed during the winter months, but then we should not allow them to continue breeding in the summer. The hatching period is about twelve days; the young leave the nest after about eighteen days, but they will still be fed by their parents for about another twenty days. Cut mealworms and other food rich in protein is absolutely necessary at this time. The hens are generally weaker than the cocks, so that the aviculturist should keep an eye out for egg binding. It is certainly best to wait a year after buying a couple before allowing them to breed, so that all this unpleasantness is avoided.

The fairly expensive but nonetheless interesting bird for beginners is the DARK FIREFINCH (*Lagonosticta rubricata*) from southeastern Africa. The hen lays four or five, sometimes six, eggs that are hatched in about two weeks (sometimes less—eleven days minimum). These birds usually use a nesting box. They may also build a bullet-shaped nest in a dense bush quite close to the ground. In order to promote successful breeding results, both parents and later the young will need to have an ample supply of insects made available to them. While the cock is singing pleasantly, he spreads his tail out like a Chinese fan.

The GREEN AVADAVAT (*Amandava formosa*) is in plentiful

supply lately. These little birds come from central India. They usually lay five eggs in a bullet-shaped nest and will certainly breed if their aviary offers the necessary privacy. The rest of its care parallels that of the well-known red avadavat.

The RED AVADAVAT (*Amandava amandava*) is from India, Assam, Cochin China, Siam, Molucca and probably also Java. There is a variety in China which has even more vivid red coloring. The female lays six to eight eggs in a little nest made of long fibers, hair, feathers and grass. They will usually use nesting boxes in the aviary, but they also like to build a nest in a dense bush. The cock builds the nest by himself, but the hen will set the eggs for eleven or twelve days; in the meantime, the fiery cock will defend his castle valiantly against all inquisitive eyes! After about twenty days the young will fly out of the nest. Their beaks are still black at that time. The coloring changes start at around three weeks. After about nine weeks the new coloring is completed, but the birds will not

*Green Avadavat (*Amandava formosa*)*

really attain their true, full coloring until after two years. During these two years there are still some remarkable observations to be made, namely, that the original coloring often still shows many variations, so that different parts of the body may be red, yellow, brown or white; only after two years will the color remain fast. The red avadavat can be quite troublesome toward other birds during the breeding period, so that it is advisable to house them separately during this time. Many fanciers allow the parents (once the chicks have hatched and the family occupies the aviary by themselves) to fly loose outside to search for insects. If we would rather play it completely safe, it is wise to give them twigs (*e.g.,* from a rose bush or from an elder tree)

*The Dark Firefinch (*Lagonosticta rubricata*)*

47

infested with leaf lice on a regular basis; the birds will enjoy these twigs thoroughly.

The colorful little GOLDEN BREASTED WAXBILL *(Amandava subflava)* from Africa, north of the Sahara, is another excellent choice for beginners. They do, however, require supplemental feeding in the form of insects and weed seeds. Even then, breeding results are precarious at best. A rather pleasant observation to be made with this species is that the

The Orange-cheeked Waxbill *(*Estrilda melpoda*)*.

parents usually relieve each other of 'hatching duty' quite accurately every two hours. The hen lays three or four eggs.

The ORANGE-CHEEKED WAXBILL *(Estrilda melpoda)* from West Africa is another quick and cute little bird. The hen usually lays four, sometimes seven, eggs which are deposited into an oval nest that has a little tunnel-like entrance. In the aviary they often like to use closed or half-open nesting boxes, in which they build a ball-shaped structure. They use little feathers, grass, wool and horse hair as nesting material. Grit and calcium are musts for this species.

The well-known and very active little RED-EARED WAXBILL *(Estrilda troglodytes)* hails from West Africa from Senegambia to the Niger and in particular from the eastern parts of North Africa. The clutch consists of four eggs that are hatched by both sexes (twelve days). They require a lot of insect food and fresh bathing water daily.

The BLACK-HEADED WAXBILL *(Estrilda atricapilla)* from Africa is quite popular presently and requires the same care as the tiny species we have just discussed.

The BLOOD-RED WAXBILL *(Lagonosticta larvata)* from northwestern Africa is a gorgeous bird. Both parents take turns in sitting on the five eggs, but at night they spend it cozily together on the nest, which is made of wood, blades of grass, coconut fibers, etc.; the nest is located low in the bushes, as well as in canary nests and nesting boxes. Insects and direct replacements of these are absolutely essential both during and outside of the breeding season.

The well-known ST. HELENA WAXBILL *(Estrilda astrild)* has some five subspecies and is found in South Africa, Matabeleland, Madagascar, Mauritius, St. Helena and New Caledonia, with cousins living in southwest Africa, Cameroon, Loano, Nubia and Zambesia. Sometimes these birds lay only one egg; at other times they may lay five or more, but then one must assume that more than one hen is using the same nest. In the aviary, the cock builds a bullet-shaped nest from grass and straw, primarily by himself. It is generally well-concealed in a thick bush. They will also use nesting boxes, which we should hang high up. After about ten days the young are hatched, and another two weeks later they fly out of the nest. Nevertheless, the parents continue to actively feed them for quite some time. Insects and soaked seeds are necessary, while bathing is essential to them (and this basically applies to all waxbills). During the breeding period it is best to house just one pair in an aviary to avoid troubles.

For those who can afford it, the following are a few more expensive species that will do very well in a community aviary together with the species already discussed. I am speaking here of three parrot-finches, namely the BLUE-FACED PARROT-FINCH (*Erythrura trichroa*) from the Caroline Is. and New Guinea, the RED-HEADED PARROT-FINCH (*E. psittacea*), and the PINTAILED NONPAREIL (*E. prasina*) from Indonesia. These birds require a roomy aviary and a lot of insects, in addition to the following: millet, oats, cracked corn, rice (also soaked in water), bread crumbs, soaked bread, greens and weed seeds. If the aviary offers enough little sheltered spots and is absolutely wind- and draft-free, the birds can stay outdoors during the winter. They are generally very active birds, particularly when we place more than one hen together with a cock.

The very expensive CRIMSON FINCH (*Poephila phaeton*) from northern Australia and Queensland will quite often earn back their cost for you, providing we supply them with a menu rich in insects and variable in seeds. In other words, they are fairly good breeders.

The DIAMOND SPARROW (*Zonaeginthus guttatus*) from eastern Australia almost always breeds in (especially low in) the nests of birds of prey. They also build bullet-shaped, free standing nests. The hen lays five or six eggs that are hatched by both sexes after a period of twelve to fourteen days. These birds will only breed in an aviary that has thick, lush greenery.

The GOULDIAN FINCH (*Chloebia gouldiae*) from northwestern Australia is a much kept and bred species, but I feel it is a little difficult for the beginner. Those that are interested, nevertheless, should refer to *All About Finches*, by Harman and Vriends. The same applies to the MASKED FINCH (*Poephila personata*) from northern and

The Red-eared Waxbill (Estrilda troglodytes).

northwestern Australia, and the PARSON FINCH *(Poephila cincta)* from the eastern regions of northwestern Australia. The very well-known LONG-TAILED GRASSFINCH *(Poephila acuticauda)* is also from the eastern part of northwestern Australia. It is interesting to note that there is a cousin species that lives in the western part of this habitat and has darker coloring and a red beak *(Poephila hecki)*. If we would like to achieve really good breeding results, we should keep these birds in separate aviaries with a lot of dense greenery and a menu that offers a great deal of variety. You should keep an eye out that the hens, which are quite eager to breed, do not become eggbound.

Requiring care that is quite different both in and out of the breeding season are the SHARP-TAILED MUNIA *(Lonchura acuticauda)* and the STRIATE MUNIA *(Lonchura striata),* which certainly stand out with their lancet-shaped tails. These birds come from India, Indonesia and New Guinea and can be considered the ancestors of the well-known Bengalese. Their breeding cycle parallels that of the little Bengalese. They must be brought indoors into a lightly heated area during the winter months and must have access to insects during the breeding period.

The BENGALESE *(Lonchura domestica)* comes in various colors, and there are even some varieties that have a little crest. These birds are suitable as both aviary and cage birds. They will even breed in a cage if it is not too small. They have developed an excellent reputation as foster parents. The young in a given brood are seldom constant in color, and many colors can be represented in just one nest. The pure white variety is quite rare, and it is difficult to breed. If a breeder has a preference for a particular color, he will need to continue breeding just that particular color from three to five times. The breeding itself does not usually pose many problems. In a well-planted aviary or in a box cage one can usually achieve very satisfactory results. However, do not disturb the breeding birds, even if they are known as birds that allow regular nest inspections, because you may well be disappointed. In order for a brood to be reared successfully, peace is a definite condition. Supply them with ample nesting boxes and nesting material (preferably half open nesting boxes 25 x 25 x 25 cm and coconut fibers and grass as

Parson Finch
(Poephila cincta)

building materials) because some birds simply allow other more aggressive birds to take an unfair share of these materials. If we have an aviary, however, that has a well-selected population (preferably small exotics), not much can go wrong; in fact, if we do not put a stop to it ourselves, a couple often does not know 'when to quit'—and that is not good either. We should not allow more than four broods per year. It is best to avoid winter breeding. A large clutch, of perhaps ten or more eggs indicates that your 'couple' is really two hens; two cocks may also behave like a 'couple,' but obviously the lack of eggs will give their little game away! A normal couple will have a clutch of five to seven eggs that are hatched in about eighteen days by both parents. After another twenty days the young fly out of the nest. They will still spend the next few nights in the parental nest. Eight to ten days after the young have come out of the eggs you could ring them in lieu of keeping well-organized records and try to keep your birds as purely heritable (homozygous) as possible. When the young are no longer being fed by their parents (after about 40 days), we remove them and place them in a large box cage. The males should be separated from the females during the winter. Young birds should not be used for breeding until they are at least one year of age. Bengalese tend to have very fast-growing nails, so we should have some flagstones present in the aviary to serve as nail files! They require fresh bathing water daily, as well as a varied tropical seed mix and insects (and direct replacements of these). Bengalese are excellent for all

kinds of crossbreeding; the resultant hybrids often win high awards at the bird shows.

The AFRICAN SILVERBILL (*Lonchura cantans*) and the INDIAN SILVERBILL (*Lonchura malabarica malabarica*) from northwestern Africa, and India, Sri Lanka, Pakistan, Afghanistan and Nepal respectively, are also beautiful birds for beginners. The African silverbills lay a clutch of

Grey-headed Silverbill (*Lonchura griseicapilla*)

three to five eggs in a little structure they build themselves, or in a deserted weaver nest. The hatching period is eleven days. After three weeks the young leave the nest. After about 50 days the young can no longer be distinguished from their parents. African silverbills are excellent foster parents and will do very well in a fairly peaceful aviary. During the winter we should take them indoors and place them in an unheated area. The Indian silverbills, which are also adorable chatterboxes like their cousins, usually have larger clutches (six to eight, sometimes ten eggs). In the wild sometimes two clutches can be found in one nest.

The SPICE BIRD *(Lonchura punctulata)* from India, Sri Lanka and around Sydney (Australia) since 1942, stands out because of the soft song of the male, with the head held high and puffed throat

The Tri-colored Munia's claws grow at a rapid rate and require frequent clipping.

feathers. It is a pity that one can hardly hear anything of their song. The hens have a tendency to suffer from egg binding, so a careful control is essential. We can keep the birds in excellent health by giving them many

insects, weed seeds and tropical seeds, some cod-liver oil and stale bread soaked in milk or water. Their clutch consists of five to seven, sometimes ten eggs.

The BLACK-HEADED MUNIA *(Lonchura atricapilla)*, the TRI-COLORED MUNIA *(Lonchura malacca)* and the WHITE-HEADED MUNIA *(Lonchura maja)* will only breed very sporadically. Sometimes they will use the deserted nests of canaries or finches and then only when the aviary offers lush greenery, especially in the form of reeds and corn. We should have a few flagstones on the aviary floor to act as manicurists (sorry, pedicurists!) and keep their nails in shape. The birds will not tolerate inspections during the breeding cycle. Supply them with perches located high up in the aviary and give them plenty of insects, cuttlebone, weed seeds, universal food, greens, canary chick rearing food and stale bread soaked in milk or water.

The JAVA SPARROW *(Padda oryzivora)* from Indonesia and St. Helena is currently a real 'in' bird! Several mutations have already been developed. The white and brown mutations have already gained quite a following, and in 1973 I came across a black-headed Java sparrow belonging to the well-known Belgian ornithologist Remi Ceuleers in Herentals. These birds are ideal aviary inhabitants. They prefer using half open nesting boxes (30 x 25 x 25 cm) or beechwood blocks (the entrance hole should have a diameter of 5 cm). If we do not do anything to avoid it, the birds will breed throughout the year, which of course could lead to egg binding problems. We should limit the breeding period

Java Sparrow
(Padda oryzivora)

to May through July and no more than four clutches per season. The hatching period is twelve to fifteen days. If the aviary is fairly peaceful, with only a few fellow inhabitants, success is guaranteed. Do not hang the breeding boxes too close together in order to avoid fighting. The prior species' feeding requirements can be referred to, since they parallel those required by the Java sparrow.

The ZEBRA FINCH *(Poephila guttata castanotis)* from Australia is a must for everyone's aviary! They are valiant, quick, little birds, and the cock's trumpeting can be heard almost all the time. Their clutch consists of four to seven white eggs. The hatching period is twelve or thirteen days. Both partners take turns in hatching the eggs. After some 21 days the young leave the nest, but they will return to the nest a good many times to spend the night or simply to have a little rest. Three weeks after the young have flown out they can be considered to be independent and can be taken away from their parents, so that the mother can start on a new round. To avoid egg binding and weak young, the number of broods should be limited to four per season. Young hens should not be used for breeding until they are at least nine months of

Only the male Cut-throat Finch possesses the red throat.

age. The cocks and hens should be separated during the winter, preferably housed indoors in an unheated but frost-free area.

The CUT-THROAT FINCH *(Amadina fasciata)* from Africa is another excellent bird for the beginner. When kept alone in a reasonably roomy aviary, we can count on breeding results. When kept in community aviaries, however, they disturb other breeding couples, so that not much good comes of both their own clutches and those of other couples. They will steal less from other birds' nests when extra material is deposited in the aviary. It is rather noteworthy that when the cock takes over the task of sitting on the eggs, he almost always has a blade of grass or straw in his beak with which he waves to his spouse as if it is a relief sign.

If you have a roomy aviary and you are fond of color and lovely nests, then I heartily recommend the following weavers *(Pyromelana* or *Euplectes)*: the NAPOLEON WEAVER *(P.* or *E. afra)* from West Africa, the GRENADIER WEAVER *(P.* or *E. oryx oryx)* from South Africa, and the ORANGE BISHOP *(E. o*

*Orange Bishop
(E. o. franciscana)*

54

franciscana) from West and East Africa. The cocks wear striking black, yellow and orange colors during the mating and breeding season; the female wears a rather drab, sparrow-like plumage, and it is difficult to tell the hens apart. If we keep more than one hen together with one cock, breeding results will certainly not be out of the question. These birds are fairly sensitive to drastic temperature changes. We should plant corn, reeds, young acacias and the like, in their aviary. Insects are essential, as are fruits and greens.

Parakeets and parrots (Psittacidae) are birds that are currently really enjoying the limelight. Our coverage of several groups of birds that are of interest to the beginner would not be complete without this very popular group, even though there is a good deal of literature available on them on the market. These hook-beaked feathered friends stand out primarily because of their strong, hook-shaped, short beaks that have bare skin at the root of the beak around the nostrils. Another of their trademarks is that each foot has two toes directed toward the front and two toes toward the back. They generally do not walk all that well as a consequence, but they make up for this by being excellent climbers, using their beaks to aid them. There are at least 600 species to be found in four of the five continents (not in Europe). Exceptions confirm the rule, but their voices are generally rather raw and ill-sounding. Their main course is fleshy fruits and berries; some species, however, have root bulbs as their main dish

which they dig out of the ground themselves, while a few species give their preference to insects and of course grass and weed seeds.

Except for the monk parakeet, they do not build a nest, at least not one that deserves the name; instead, they generally choose a tree hollow or fork and line it with some nesting material. They usually lay few eggs, which are white, and they will breed several times per season.

The colorful JANDAYA CONURE *(Aratinga jandaya)* comes from South America. Each bird is very attached to its mate. They can be unbelievably

Jandaya Conures are avid gnawers and should be supplied with branches and twigs.

destructive, particularly when kept in an aviary that is partially or completely constructed of wood. The three to four eggs are hatched by both the cock and hen, and whichever bird is not sitting on the nest will aggressively guard the immediate surroundings. Under the circumstances, I feel it is best to house these birds either in a very roomy community aviary (with parakeet species of the same size) or in an aviary by themselves.

No doubt you know the SCARLET MACAW *(Ara macao),* which comes from Mexico south to Panama, Colombia, Ecuador, Bolivia, the Amazon region and the Guianas, from your visits to the zoo. A few are kept by individual fanciers as well. Their screeching is deafening, but young birds can be made very tame and will then rarely screech. When they are angry, however, they can be a little dangerous with their sturdy beaks! Because of the fact that they eat fruit, various cultured seeds, grain, etc., they are considered very destructive in their country of origin. In the aviary these seeds should be a permanent part of their menu, in addition to corn, soaked vegetables (carrots, lettuce, endives, etc), buds and twigs, rusks, sunflower seeds, rice and grass seeds. Various other species of *Ara* are regularly offered for sale on the market and require similar care.

With the exception of the MASKED LOVEBIRD *(Agapornis personata personata),* the ABYSSINIAN LOVEBIRD *(Agapornis taranta)* and the

The Scarlet Macaw achieves a length of 85 cm.

Peach-faced Lovebirds are naturally active and profit from larger enclosures.

PEACH-FACED LOVEBIRD

(Agapornis roseicollis), the care and breeding of lovebirds *(Agapornis),* is not such a simple matter. Their nutritional requirements are seeds, oats, rice, young buds and twigs, egg, rusks, fruit, ant eggs and other insects. For breeding purposes we supply them with a wooden box 15 x 15 x 25 cm high, with an entrance hole that has a diameter of 6 cm. This box must be kept moist, and it is wise to hang it in the open part of the aviary so that it will receive an occasional rain shower. During dry spells you should keep the nesting box wet by regularly using your garden hose set at a weak drizzle. An interesting habit peculiar to various species of lovebirds is that they place their building materials, in the form of grass, straw, etc., in between their tail feathers, or more accurately, in between the feathers of the rump and back, and bring them in this fashion to the nest. For those of you who are particularly interested in these really fascinating birds, please refer to *The Handbook of Lovebirds* (T.F.H. Publications, Inc., Neptune, New Jersey).

The RINGNECK PARAKEET *(Psittacula krameri)* from India and Africa is another very good choice for beginners. The female lays three to five eggs which she hatches by herself. The cock feeds her on the nest. The breeding season usually takes place quite early in the year, but personally I feel the best months are March to July. The young come out of the nest after six weeks. There is a yellow variety also, which is the so-called lutino ringneck parakeet.

The beautifully colored REGENT PARROT *(Polytelis anthopeplus)* from southern and western Australia is a sweet-natured bird and is also that way

Ring-neck Parakeet (Psittacula krameri)

Regent Parrot
(Polytelis anthopeplus)

toward the small exotics; they are not always as pleasant toward their own kind, so that it is advisable to keep just one pair of them in an aviary. The hen generally lays four eggs; although in the wild she usually lays more (six). In the wild they like to treat themselves to honeycomb and blossom petals. Seeds and fresh buds are also welcome. They prefer to build their nest in a tree hollow, particularly in trees along large rivers.

BROWN'S ROSELLA *(Platycercus venustus)* and other rosella species (which come from Australia) are certainly for our beginners who can afford them. Brown's rosella lives in large flocks (about ten pairs), but during the breeding season they split up into pairs. Successful breeding can be achieved in the aviary, but special literature would be required, as the procedure is much too involved and lengthy to discuss here. So if one would really like to breed these species, detailed literature is absolutely essential.

Everyone is familiar with the BUDGERIGAR *(Melopsittacus undulatus).* Its origin stems particularly from the interior of Australia. Their clutch consists of three or four eggs, but in captivity it may consist of five to eight eggs, sometimes even more. They are most fertile toward the end of their second and the beginning of their third year of life. Females that are older than six should no longer be permitted to breed, because the resultant young are much too weak. The hatching period is sixteen to eighteen days. The female generally hatches the eggs by herself, but the cock guards the nest and brings food to his mate. The young leave the nest after about one month. They will retain their youth's plumage for another six to eight weeks. The permanent coloring process is completed after some six to nine months. Budgerigars breed several times per year, but more than three or four clutches is not advisable since there is a very good chance that some of the young in the later clutches will have crooked feet or toes, poor wings, insufficient feathering, etc.; the hen is not strong enough to actively feed and take care of them.

The GREATER SULPHUR-CRESTED COCKATOO *(Cacatua galerita galerita)* from Australia and Tasmania is also a bird that practically everyone knows. These birds, that are usually kept in

Brown's Rosella (Platycercus venustus) is also known as Northern Rosella. These birds grow to a length of 28 cm.

cages or on a perch stand, will come to breed in a large aviary. The female lays two eggs that are hatched after a full month. After ten weeks the young leave the nest and after eleven weeks they are independent. Supplemental nutrition in the form of food rich in eggs is necessary. Many specimens can be taught quite a respectable vocabulary

SWAINSON'S BLUE MOUNTAIN LORIKEET *(Trichoglossus haematodus)* from Australia, the Moluccas, Tasmania and New Guinea is a very colorful bird. The clutch consists of two, sometimes four, eggs. The hen hatches alone. The young leave the nest after 50 or 60 days. After about six months the young will start to assume their adult coloring. The nesting boxes must be very roomy: 28 x 28 x 35 cm. high, with an entrance hole that has a 10 cm diameter. We should keep these birds in a separate aviary, because they are generally intolerant toward both fellow species and other birds. When kept alone, however, they become very attached to their keeper and will even learn to speak a few words. If we wish to book success with breeding efforts, we should feed the young with milk, white bread soaked in water or milk, pound cake soaked in milk, corn, grain, greens and universal food in which we have mixed a little sugar. By offering them a little hemp we can prevent the rather watery droppings from becoming too thin.

THIS MONTH IN YOUR AVIARY

In the following pages I will attempt to give an overall view of the most important duties that we should fulfill each month to guarantee the very best of care for our birds. We do not pretend to have covered all the bases, but it should give you a fair idea as to what will be required month by month during the various seasons of the year. We do feel that it would make sense to group the birds according to the most popular collections kept by beginning bird enthusiasts.

JANUARY

EXOTICS: This is the ideal time to start looking into bringing breeding boxes and the like into order for the upcoming breeding season.

Not all small tropical and sub-tropical birds use nesting boxes, but we are certainly wise to offer

the widest range in styles—that is, both closed and half-open nesting boxes. We keep in mind that we should always offer twice as many breeding facilities as there are couples; in other words, if we have ten couples, we should hang twenty nesting boxes. Red-eared waxbills, red avadavats, orange-cheeked waxbills, zebra finches, Bengalese and the like, like to use nesting boxes (both open and closed), but they might also use old nests that were made by other birds or build one themselves. This is another reason why we should prune our aviary shrubbery religiously and in such a way so that when the leaves come back on the shrubs, plenty of little 'forks' will result. We should not prune the bushes to the point where they are too 'open' and will not provide enough natural protection.

We should also watch out for perches. An aviary that has some bushes and shrubs will provide plenty of natural perches, particularly if we have done enough pruning. However, the artificial perches that we provide for our birds should not be too thin; otherwise, they will not help keep down nail growth and allow the birds to rest properly. When we say "not too thin" we understand this to mean that a bird's foot should not be able to entirely encircle the perch. The round perches available on the market are fine, but we would do well to flatten the tops a little. Munias, spice birds, African silverbills, grass finches and parakeets prefer the flattened

Breeding boxes mounted on the outside of the aviary saves space and facilitates easy access for nest checks.

Various types of breeding boxes.

tops in particular. Naturally, everything must be very clean and disinfected. This is particularly important for our smaller birds, especially if we would like to motivate them to breed. With larger birds we should also be sure that there are enough (usually half-open) nesting boxes. Some of them, such as the indigo bunting, cardinals, silver-eared mesia, nightingales, etc. will build their own free-standing nests.

We should pay extra attention to nesting materials which are available to us at this time. Some of the materials that would be suitable are dry grass, moss, hay, leaves, spider webs, string (hemp) and the like. We cannot use wool, cotton strips and scraps of newspaper, to mention just a few. These materials do not provide enough ventilation; because of the numerous droppings that some birds 'stick' to the edge of the nest, ventilation is, of course, very important.

If we breed birds in cages and/or vitrines the same guidelines apply. However, I would like to add an additional important point in this regard: reed stalks and flagstones are absolutely necessary when housing munias and spice birds. The thrush species (such as the white-crested thrush, the babblers, red-legged thrush) also need plenty of perches, both the natural and artificial variety (diameter about 4 cm).

I would also like to point out at this time that your bird collection should be well chosen from a scientific viewpoint. The reader may well be aware of the fact, as an example, that the white-crested thrush we just mentioned likes to consume little birds! We can assume from this that we'd better not house it together with smaller species! A general guideline is that most little birds can be kept together, but even here there are some exceptions; sometimes there are a few birds in a group that are particularly aggressive and can be a real nuisance for the breeding couples. The cut-throat finches, olive and Cuban finches and mannikins come to mind in this regard. When the time comes for hanging up the nesting boxes, this should also be done with a good deal of consideration, because it

Ventilation holes should be drilled into the sides of the nesting box.

often happens that little birds desert their broods out of sheer fear and nerves, generally caused by the fact that the various nesting boxes are hung too close together. It is also no luxury to hang them somewhat hidden behind bushes, etc., and this applies to both an outdoor and indoor aviary.

Waxbills and Indian silverbills, to mention two examples, are alarmed by almost anything and will then desert the nest or brood, and they are very unlikely to return to it. So as we already mentioned, the nesting boxes should not be hung too close together; a distance of 60 cm. between each should be considered the minimum, if we are to avoid internal strife (I am thinking in particular of the long-tailed grassfinch).

BUDGERIGARS: Our beechwood blocks and other nesting boxes must be absolutely clean and disinfected. We should be sure that several ventilation holes have been drilled into the sides. The same applies for the lovebirds group. We would add here, though, that the budgerigars should not be too young; that is, at least eight or nine months old if we want to count on healthy young babies. It would be even better to wait until the would-be parents are one year of age. Now that we are speaking of suitable ages, this is a good time to add the following: our tropical and sub-tropical birds should be at least nine months old in order to have reasonable chances for successful breeding results. The same applies to our large parakeet and parrot varieties.

It is not a simple matter to motivate your wild birds to breed;

it is not everyone's forte! Most wild birds do not use nesting boxes, but since crossbreeding is quite possible with canaries, we would need to use little nesting boxes if we use a canary hen. In any event, this month you can start to collect the nesting material already mentioned and lay it out to dry (perhaps in an attic room), so that you will have both a sufficient amount and the right kind of building materials when the breeding season is upon us.

FEBRUARY

EXOTICS: It is generally a good idea to bring all the exotic birds indoors for the winter months; at least we will then avoid the chance of sooner or later finding some victims of the colder weather. It would be ideal, of course, if we have a lightly heated location in which to house them. Those birds that have an Australian ancestry, such as the parrot finches and the various waxbills (I am thinking in particular of the star finch, the Sydney waxbill, the diamond sparrow, etc.) of course are better able to handle the cold than birds that hail from Africa or tropical America.

Here again, putting together couples is an area that requires our foremost attention. Since it is a difficult task to distinguish between the sexes of various species, we must already start in February with the selection of birds.

Pay special attention to the behavior of the birds; in species where the sexes are identical in coloring, the cock will sing, dance or court his future bride in some other manner. Keep in mind that masked finches need to have charcoal available to them as

soon as the breeding season commences; collecting it may be seen as a pleasant activity for this month! If we wish to enhance our chances of success in breeding munias, we will need to take a very close look at the greenery in our aviary, as we already mentioned in the previous month. You will need, as an example, to see if you can get some reed bushes, since quite a few species of munias will nestle in them; this plant will also help in keeping down nail growth, as you already know. It is still very difficult to distinguish between the sexes of the red avadavats. It is only just before the breeding season starts

Black-throated Munia
(Lonchura malacca ferruginosa)

(end of March) that the cock takes on his beautiful red coloring.

ZEBRA FINCHES: The zebra finches, of course, should also not yet be spurred to breed; it is still much too early. If we wish to breed birds well, we should wait until mid-March before bringing the hens and cocks together. Only towards the end of March or the beginning of April do we start supplying the birds with nesting material so that they can start building. I would suggest four clutches per year as the maximum. This is not just a figure snatched out of mid-air, but a guideline that I personally adhere to after years of experimentation. It is never a good idea to abuse your birds by allowing them to have too many broods. Keep in

Although similar in appearance to the male, the female Long-tailed Grassfinch has a narrower and smaller throat patch.

mind, always one, three or more couples together.

GRASS FINCHES: These mostly gorgeous birds must be acclimated with the utmost care. The pintailed nonpareil, for example, requires very detailed care. Acclimatization is only met with success by the more experienced fancier. So during the winter, keep them inside at temperatures that never near the freezing point. Japanese nightingales can remain outdoors; after all, in their homeland they must also put up with some pretty cold winters. If they can be brought indoors, so much the better; no point in taking unnecessary risks. Olive finches should only be placed with somewhat larger birds; the Cuban finch, in particular, can tend to be a bit difficult sometimes. Keep this in mind when selecting a collection of birds. Rainbow buntings and Mexican nonpareils are good breeders and can even be tamed; they are generally quite a lot cheaper to buy in the winter months, which is the reason why I am mentioning them here.

BUDGERIGARS: It is getting near the time to start pairing up your birds for the upcoming breeding season. Armed with the pairing schedules we can start making our combination choices. And now that we have plenty of time, we can also devote some thought to speech lessons. I am sure you know that budgerigars learn to speak quite readily. A woman's voice, however, is the most suitable for giving speech lessons.

We can update our breeding records at this time, so that we will not land in difficulties during the breeding season.

WILD BIRDS: The cage birds that we can keep in our aviary also require some special attention, particularly during the winter months. We should give them seeds rich in fats; hang a

THE WORLD'S LARGEST SELECTION OF PET, ANIMAL, AND MUSIC BOOKS.

T.F.H. Publications publishes more than 900 books covering many hobby aspects (dogs, cats, birds, fish, small animals, music, etc.). Whether you are a beginner or an advanced hobbyist you will find exactly what you're looking for among our complete listing of books. For a free catalog fill out the form on the other side of this page and mail it today.

. . . **BIRDS** . .

. . **CATS** . . .

. . . **ANIMALS** . . .

. . . **DOGS** . . .

. . **FISH** . . .

. . . **MUSIC** . . .

*Male budgerigars have blue ceres, the
female a light pinkish one.*

seed bell in the aviary, because
you probably know that your wild
birds can be left outdoors
providing they have a good
shelter. It is especially at this time
that we should give them an
occasional treat, such as grass
and weed seeds that are available
in every good bird store.

Providing our birds with a
really good seed mixture and
grass meal will help our birds get
the red back in their plumage
after the molt. During the entire
year we should offer them pine
branches and the like, complete
with bark, which will also
stimulate the red to return after
the molt.

CANARIES: Especially those
canaries that are kept in a
moderately heated area can be
quite restless at this time; some
hens even fly around this month

with pieces of straw or little
feathers in their beaks! Naturally,
we will have to contain this desire
to breed as much as we can. A
colder area, with no males
present, is best for the hens at
this time. From this you have
already surmised that the hens
and cocks are separated during
the winter. When they are not
separated, the cocks start
pursuing the hens much too early
so that they do not have ample
opportunity to gather strength for
the upcoming season. We should
give the hens an extra dish with a
treat, some cod-liver oil and a
good brand of universal food
during the winter. We should keep
an eye on their overall
appearance too. Once we start
with the breeding, both cocks and
hens should look impeccable. Any
dirt at the feet, bill or wings can
be washed off with lukewarm
water (this also applies to other
birds). If the nails are too long,
they should be carefully trimmed.

MARCH

EXOTICS: Not all of our tropical birds require the same nesting materials. This is a point we should definitely keep in mind. The following materials are always suitable: winter grass, moss, hay and anything that has been noted under the month of January. Red avadavats use feathers quite often, while goat hair is used by the white-rumped shama. The starling and troupial species (such as the military starling, pagoda starling and splendid glossy starling) use all kinds of building materials.

Supplemental nutrition requires our special attention at this time of year. Townsend's solitaire, as an example, must have a lot of fruit (raisins, bananas, berries, apples and pears), while the occipital bluepie loves raw red meat or a dead mouse; then again, the tanagers really enjoy stale white bread soaked in honey! The main fare for our grass finches is insects and universal food (that would also apply to the rainbow bunting and such).

Nesting location is another point for consideration. Spice birds and munias will only achieve good breeding results when they are not disturbed. Pick a corner of the aviary and plant some reeds, in which we can then hang a few small nests. Weavers are another group of birds that will be very pleased to have reeds in the aviary.

If we wish to breed the paradise whydah, our aviary will need to be very peaceful indeed, with only a pair of melba finches or Wiener's waxbills as co-inhabitants, if possible (they are quite expensive) perhaps a couple of each. Paradise whydahs are

For successful pairings special attention must be paid to the diet before and during the breeding season.

similar to the cuckoo in that they lay their eggs in the nests of the birds just mentioned. Those of us who are more limited in funds may well try breeding—often with success—the St. Helena waxbills and firefinches. If we have pintailed whydahs the same rules apply. The red-eared waxbill can also be of use here.

ZEBRA FINCHES: March is also a good time to start the breeding cycle with our little zebras. Place at least three pairs together in an aviary. To ensure that the breeding couples will stay together, we can place the cock and hen together in a small cage for two weeks. Experience has taught us that the first brood will in any event produce pure young. Chances of this happening with the second round are already considerably reduced, since the cock will then also be paying some attention to other hens; if we have pure heritable (homozygous) birds of the same coloring and markings this does not matter, but if we have various colors together in one aviary, then the young cannot be considered pure. For nesting material we try to offer somewhat elastic material; no cotton, newspaper, etc. Hay and winter grass would be better. The bird droppings are 'stored' on the edge of the nest so that a little ventilation is no great luxury. Do not use hens that are younger than ten months; hens that are too young tend to suffer a lot from egg binding. Do not keep a second male, as this is also likely to cause problems. Mix a little cod-liver oil in with the seed (three to five drops per kilo of seed) and do not forget to offer your birds plenty of greens, cuttlebone and grit. This notation would also apply for our other birds. When the young zebra finches are independent, at about ten days after they have flown out, they should be removed from the aviary or breeding cage.

BUDGERIGARS: The best breeding box for a parakeet is a right-angled box measuring at least 20 x 15 x 15 cm. A roomy beechwood box would also be suitable. As nesting materials we supply them with some woodchips which they will sometimes use but which we can better deposit into the nesting boxes ourselves. Breeding results are most likely to occur in an outdoor aviary; the breeding boxes are best placed in the covered section, but not in the shelter! On the floor of the breeding box we place a small plank of not too hard wood, preferably under the entrance hole. Next to this plank we carve out a round, not too deep nesting

cup with a diameter of about 10 cm.

In mid-March we can bring the breeding pairs together. Here again, do not use birds that are too young. By the same token, cocks and hens that are too old

Zebra Finches are prolific breeders.

should not be used either. If we keep budgerigars together with other birds, we must be sure that the number of nesting boxes far exceeds the number of couples, so that there is plenty of choice for the various birds. Independent young should be removed from the aviary.

LARGE PARAKEETS: Our lovebirds require special breeding boxes which we must keep moist. As nesting material we offer strips of bark from willow trees, fruit trees, the elder, etc. The branches or twigs can also be placed in the aviary; the birds will then tear off strips of bark themselves. It is best to house

Peach-faced Lovebirds (Agapornis roseicollis)

only one couple per aviary or else fighting is quite likely to occur. The monk parakeet is virtually the only parakeet that builds its own nest, and quite a complicated one at that. Plenty of wood, twigs, grass, etc. are therefore necessary. Jandaya conures, white-eared conures and similar birds require nesting blocks of at least 20 x 30 x 30 cm. This is the time to breed for Bourke's parrots. Give them plenty of fresh twigs from the willow and beech trees; fruits and fresh mealworms are also necessary in their diet.

CANARIES: At the end of this month most canary fanciers randomly place their selected males and females together. However, since the males are usually ready for mating earlier than the females (in most cases), some wild pursuits and fights are not unlikely. It is better, therefore, to place the hen in the breeding location first, along with plenty of

nesting material, preferably winter grass cut short since this is still readily available to us. Winter grass is grass that was not previously mowed and that has dried. When the year has progressed just a little farther, the grass will start growing again, so this is the time to pick it. The cock should be placed in a different cage next to the breeding cage. He should not be placed together with the hen until she starts making a nest, which is the sign that she is ready for breeding. After the first egg has been laid, the cock is returned to his own cage or placed with a different hen if we are using the alternate breeding system.

APRIL

Thrush-type birds, such as the dyal thrush and white-rumped shama should be given mealworms, ant eggs, spiders, beetles and a good brand of universal food on a regular basis during the breeding season. Because of their lively nature, it is wise to house them separately in an aviary that is not too petite in its dimensions and has plenty of lush greenery. Japanese nightingales absolutely need a water bath available to them during the breeding period.

Large nesting boxes that have been filled with coarser materials are necessary for the pagoda starling. In addition to chick rearing food and insects, they need soaked raisins if we hope to achieve success in the breeding department. The same is also required by Townsend's solitaire, which has quite a lot in common with our canary. We should keep an ultra-clean aviary floor for our tanagers. Refresh the floor every other day as a minimum—

preferably every day. The Brazilian tanager breeds well in captivity. Extra insects, white bread soaked in milk and honey, fruit cut into small pieces and eggs are absolutely essential. However, house them separately as they are quite rapacious.

If we would like to motivate the indigo bunting to breed, we should make a few cup-shaped nests of string, which we place in dense shrubbery about 30 cm from the ground. The Virginian cardinal is not likely to breed well unless the pair is housed in a roomy aviary by themselves. Fairly thick greenery is desirable if not essential. The hooded siskin is an excellent choice for crossbreeding with a not too large canary hen. If these two birds are separated by a wire partition, as an example, breeding results will not be too far off. As soon as they display an interest in each other they can be placed together in a small aviary that has a generous amount of bushes; for the rest of it we can act as though they are a pair of canaries.

The gray singing finch can be motivated to breed by hanging a few nesting boxes up high in the aviary. Cordon bleus will not give us any difficulties providing the aviary is located in peaceful surroundings and does not house too many large birds.

The same applies to the orange-cheeked waxbills, red-eared waxbills, etc. These species need hair and wool for nesting material.

One final note: all tropical birds will usually come to breed if their aviary is endowed with good, dense shrubbery and plenty and all kinds of nesting boxes which we have hung at various elevations and at the proper distance from each other. We must never forget to provide our birds with chick rearing food, universal food, fruit, bathing water, cuttlebone, fine greens, small mushrooms (cut) and ant eggs.

ZEBRA FINCHES: Zebra finches are also known as good breeders. Still, I strongly urge you not to disturb your couples too much. Although by nature zebra finches make round, closed nests in the wild, in captivity they use pretty well all kinds of nesting boxes. However, these birds have a bad habit of closing off their first nest (complete with eggs) with a new little nest. Sometimes they may make three or four nests with eggs in them one on top of the

The female Parson Finch has a narrower and smaller throat patch.

other! Particularly when using deep nesting boxes this phenomenon is not that unusual; with half-open nesting boxes this takes place with a great deal less frequency. But what can we do about these multi-storied nests? Fortunately, the answer is simple: we fill each deep nesting box with the proper nesting material right up until just under the nest opening (about 3 cm). Zebra finches always want to be able to look out of their nest to see what is going on about them.

Cuttlebone provides calcium for proper eggshell formation.

Consequently, they will build (and lay eggs—which could well lead to egg binding) until they have reached the nest opening. A few drops of cod-liver oil (about 5 drops per 1 kilo seed; 3 drops per 1 liter of drinking water) can do much to prevent egg binding and other such unpleasantries. Cuttlebone and greens, ant eggs and small cut mealworms must

not be forgotten. We should never allow the zebras to rear more than four broods per season. Once the young are independent, even though they have not yet achieved their adult coloring and their beaks are still partially black, we should separate them from their parents so that a new brood can be started.

BUDGERIGARS: These birds need plenty of room if we keep them outdoors in a community aviary (only with other parakeet varieties) and want them to breed. Keep an eye out that your budgerigars do not start teasing other, non-hook-beaked birds by hanging on their tails, inspecting their nests and stealing nesting material out of the nesting boxes being used by other birds; this is why I am not in favor of keeping budgerigars together with tropical and sub-tropical birds. However, if our aviary is really quite large, meaning that there is enough space for the birds to determine their own individual territories, these problems are not likely to occur; but there must be enough room, certainly no overpopulation and sufficient greenery. Sometimes the hens tend to be quite aggressive; if this is the case it is best to remove them from the aviary, particularly if we are trying to breed other birds besides budgerigars as well. Sometimes a couple will not breed in a breeding cage. Experience has shown that by placing an actively breeding couple together with the inactive couple, good results can often be produced. Perhaps a case of monkey do what monkey see! The 'lodging' couple, however, should have the same coloring and marking as the first pair, so that in the event that they switch partners, we do not end up with a potpourri of colors! We should also be aware of the fact that we never place new couples in an aviary where the inhabitants are already busy with nests, eggs or young, because the established population will relentlessly pursue the newcomers in such an intense and aggressive manner that several casualties are likely to result, especially among the new couples because the established aviary population will often work together with a kind of team spirit.

Oats in any form do much to stimulate the desire to mate. Of course we should not give too much . . . it must certainly not become the main fare.

WILD BIRDS: If we wish to breed our wild birds well, then of course here again we need absolute peace and quiet, just as we do with our tropical birds. The aviary should have a hedge of elder, ivy and beech, preferably growing as densely as possible. We could leave a roomy straight flying strip open at the front of the aviary, which would also allow us to enjoy a good view of our birds. A rich assortment of seeds and insects, chick rearing food, universal food and greens (e.g. lettuce, endives, chickweed and spinach) must not be forgotten. Your wild birds are most likely to breed when one couple is kept by themselves in an aviary.

If these bases are covered, not much is likely to go wrong. Keep an eye out for egg binding. If there is constant fighting it means that the aviary is either overpopulated or our collection was not properly selected. (Many fanciers add wild birds to their community aviary, together with canaries and other such birds,

Canaries prefer open nests.

which produces a very interesting aviary that certainly offers the opportunity for family enlargements.) In the event of any difficulties, we simply remove the troublemakers from the aviary. Young birds should be separated from the parents as soon as they are independent.

CANARIES: In this month most canaries are either occupied with their nests or already have their eggs. As pointed out earlier, we should remove the cock after the first egg has been laid. He should not be returned to his family until the fledglings start to make peeping sounds while being fed. So if we perceive some desperate peeping going on as soon as the hen lands on the nest's edge, we will know she is in need of help with the feeding of the chicks, and the time has come for the cock to be back with his chicks. When the hen shows breeding tendencies for the second round, the young are then at the stage where they can do without mother's part in the feeding responsibility. Hence, when the hen has one egg, the cock and the young chicks are then moved to the male's quarters. The cock then continues to feed the young—by himself now—until they are independent. During this period of having and rearing young, our birds must have a continuous choice of: 1) mixed seed; 2) egg food; 3) universal food; 4) greens (especially chickweed); 5) grit or pieces of shell from chicken eggs; 6) clean water. If you have good parent birds, then the breeding

season should go off without a hitch.

MAY
EXOTICS: In an aviary that is both large and well planted with greenery, there is, of course, room for various species of birds. Be sure that all species have access to cuttlebone, greens, universal food, chick rearing food and insects. Arabian golden sparrows feed their young primarily insects, second to germinated seeds, greens and universal food. When I speak of 'germinated seeds' I would like to add that this food is really a must for all our birds. Insects and little spiders must not be missing on the menu of blue pheasants. The young absolutely love them! Although they are mostly seed-eaters, black-headed siskins also enjoy insects during the breeding period, which they give by the 'mouthful' to their young. Gray singing finches feed their young primarily seed, which they 'soak' in their crop. Once the young have flown out at two weeks, the cock will still feed them for some time. Before they have flown out, the hen hooded siskin feeds her young, but once they have gone out of the nest, they become the cock's responsibility. Egg food, mealworms, small (fresh of course) ant eggs and some greens must not be lacking on the menu. Cuban finches cannot do without a good brand of universal food, some chick rearing food and insects, in addition, of course, to weed and grass seeds. Greens should not be left out either. You know, of course, that these birds can be let loose in

Bullfinch (Pyrrhula pyrrhula) thrives on fruits, buds, insects and seed mixes.

your garden during the time that they are feeding their young, providing they are kept in an aviary by themselves.

Our weavers are also very fond of insects and soaked seeds; in fact, without this food they will not stay alive very long. The same applies to the tanager. Hard-boiled and chopped egg is highly recommendable too. Oranges, pears, bananas and berries complete the list of nutritional requirements. Naturally, any large fruits should be cut into small pieces. Mynah birds need, in addition to fruit, insects and seed, red meat (lean chopped meat) to feed to their young. When you bring these foods to them you will see how enthusiastically they fly to them! Earthworms, ant eggs, beetles and such are also foods they like to feed their young. The same applies to all kinds of starlings. Raisins are especially appreciated by the pagoda starling. The young from the Japanese nightingale love berries, fruit, mealworms, universal and chick rearing foods, and various sorts of greens.

Thrushes (such as the dyal thrush, orange headed ground thrush, white-rumped shama) also enjoy stale bread, grated carrots, hard-boiled egg, raw or cooked lean ground meat and chick rearing food. Our smaller birds, such as the orange-cheeked waxbill, red-eared waxbill, lavender finch and such, are quite satisfied with a good seed menu, small mealworms, ant eggs, fresh greens and soaked seeds. Millet spray must not be forgotten, especially in the breeding season. Our various parrot finches must not be without charcoal, as you already know. We can buy this packaged in several forms from any good bird or pet store, so this should not pose any problems.

ZEBRA FINCHES: Zebra finches eat a great deal while in the nest. Millet is the main dish. The parent birds will make sure that it is first soaked in their crops. Stale white bread soaked in milk or water is also a favorite for feeding their young. After about 21 days, the

Orange-cheeked Waxbills.

fledglings leave the nest and will spend the initial period somewhat ill at ease on the aviary floor, still begging for food. It is heartwarming to observe that in addition to the 'real' parents, other zebra finches will bravely help in filling up the youngster's

Heck's Grassfinch can be distinguished from the Long-tailed by its red bill.

tummies—that is to say, their crops. This month we should keep a special eye out for any overly adventuresome birds that are not yet big enough but nevertheless undertake a discovery flight out of the nest to Mother Earth. If the aviary keeper does not pick them up quickly and place them back in the nest, they may quickly fall victim to cold and hunger. When placing such a bird back in its nest, you should place your hand over the nest opening for a moment until everything is quiet inside; if this is not done, there is a good chance the entire nest will take flight, and then we are in deeper trouble. Naturally, we should ring our birds; this can be done when they are eight or nine days old. Small tropical birds such as red-eared waxbills and red avadavats can, of course, also be ringed. Here again, they can be ringed after about ten days.

BUDGERIGARS: The nesting blocks, which we already know should be hung in the covered section of the outer aviary, must have a few ventilation holes; this is because of the fact that the parents sleep in the nest opening—it would not take long before all the fresh air for the young was depleted, with all the miserable consequences we can imagine.

In the breeding period they should not be wanting for cuttlebone, calcium and greens (in the form of lettuce, endives, etc.). Apart from seed, they also feed their young stale bread soaked in milk, egg food and chick rearing food. We can mix a few drops of cod-liver oil in with their seed. We will be rewarded with sturdy young and will avoid the risk that the hens succumb to egg binding. You must be sure to provide them with more than enough nesting facilities throughout the entire breeding season if you want to avoid internal strife. For good breeding results and the proper rearing of the young birds, this is absolutely essential, and we feel this cannot be emphasized enough. Do not forget, and this also applies to all of our other breeding birds, to regularly supply them with charcoal, as I have written before.

After about 30 days, the young leave the nesting boxes; they will still be fed by the cock for quite some time with the foods mentioned above. In the meantime, the hen is enthusiastically busy with her new brood. Sometimes the young are plucked bald, particularly by the hen. This is often a hereditary trait. It is best not to continue breeding with such a bird. It is not very unusual to find a misformed chick in a nest of budgerigars. This is often due to breeding too closely related birds. It is best, of course, to kill such unfortunate offspring.

LARGE PARAKEETS: What I said in the section on budgerigars also applies here: make sure there are ventilation holes in the nesting boxes. Some lovebirds love raisins and other sweet fruit. Stale brown bread soaked in milk or water is also very important for the lovebirds. A few drops of cod-liver oil—three at the most—sprinkled on this bread will do no harm. The young will become stronger from it. Greens, hard-boiled egg yolk and ant eggs are also favorite foods of various lovebird species, particularly the red-faced lovebird.

Hard-boiled eggs, seeds (sunflower seeds, hemp, millet, cracked corn) and greens are also foods eaten by the young of the monk parakeet. Fruit must not be lacking in their menu. The nanday conure's young must have calcium, a salt lick and stale white bread soaked in water or milk. Cactus conures are crazy about oats, and their young will do well on it too. The ringneck parakeet also likes rusks soaked in milk mixed with a little honey.

Also applicable to the larger parakeet varieties is that we must ensure that their young have plenty of breads, seeds, mealworms, ant eggs, greens, fresh twigs, chick rearing food, grass seeds, germinated seeds, some calcium and a salt lick.

WILD BIRDS: Practically all of your wild song birds need insect food, preferably live insects. The simplest way of fulfilling this requirement is to open your aviary door and allow the parent birds to fly loose and hunt for this food themselves. It is pleasant for the birds to be given this freedom and really be able to fly to their heart's content, and of course it is also much easier for us. When

the young start sitting on the edge of the nest and start trying out their wings, we will need to close the aviary door once again and take the responsibility of providing them with insects ourselves. Parent birds that have young in the nest keep coming back, so that there is little risk in allowing them to fly loose.

A Red-cheeked Cordonbleu (Uraeginthus bengalus) hen with her chick four days after fledging.

CANARIES: Feeding requirements of the young canaries were covered in quite some detail in the previous month. Young canaries that have recently flown out will not immediately be able to find the feed and seed dishes. Therefore, we should place a flat saucer with a little egg food and seed in the center of the sand drawer. We should not give too much egg food, since this could cause constipation. Once you see the young pecking at the seed, we should no longer offer egg food at all. Leave the cock with his young chicks as long as he still plays a part in feeding time. Once the young are independently eating from the regular seed hopper, we can catch them and place them in a separate area for the young. But do not do this too hastily.

JUNE

EXOTICS: At this time the young from the first brood have become independent. At that stage the following will require your attention: independent white-rumped shamas must be removed from their parents, otherwise the parents will not start on a new brood. The same applies to other

Some birds will benefit from a daily misting.

thrush species. Young from the Japanese nightingale and the silver-eared mesia are also best removed from their parents. Troupials should be housed by themselves, that is, without other inhabitants, because they have the unpleasant habit of destroying the nests of other birds, including fellow species. Did you know, incidentally, that a couple of pagoda starlings can be let loose

to fly in your garden when the hen has laid the first egg? Both mother and father will ambitiously seek all kinds of insects in the immediate surroundings which they will later feed to their young. Bathing water should not be forgotten during the breeding period.

You may like to try breeding a cross between a pagoda starling and an ordinary inland starling.

Bathing water should also be given to our starling species during the breeding season; your small aviary birds should also not be without it.

Now that the young have become independent, you can start with the taming of various species; I am thinking here in particular of the mynah birds. You must not forget to spray mist your tanagers daily with pure water that has been heated to room temperature. It is also best to keep Brazilian tanagers in an aviary or cage by themselves, because they are quite feisty; once the young have flown out, in particular, they do not make allowances for anyone!

Independent Cuban finches should also be removed from their parents because the cock will aggressively pursue his sons, while the hen will do the same with the daughters, which, incidentally, is quite a noteworthy trait.

ZEBRA FINCHES: Our zebras will still be fed by Tom, Dick and Harry for quite some time after they have flown out of the nest, although after a while they know quite well where to find the feeders. Once they have reached the age of 40 to 45 days, they can be considered independent. Their beaks will also betray that they are no longer attached to

Budgerigar chicks in the nesting box.

Mother's apron strings; specifically, their beaks have now changed from black to red. In another three weeks or so these zebras could, technically, be used for breeding already, but everyone will understand that this would not be very wise. A good bird breeder proceeds as follows: as soon as the young are independent and have reached their adult coloring, they are caught in their aviary or breeding cage and housed separately, in such a manner so that the cocks are separated from the hens. If we do not do this, it would not be long before one or more of them found a mate. Egg binding and other such problems would become a common occurrence, and this is hardly the idea. Young zebra finches of this breeding year should not be used for breeding sooner than the following breeding year. There should be a substantial period of time between 'becoming adult'

and 'becoming ripe' for breeding. The best length of time for this period is ten months. It is for this reason that I advise against late breeding, such as October or even later.

BUDGERIGARS: In this category of birds I would like to point out the following, although it has been brought up before, but no amount of emphasis is enough. Specifically, when budgerigars are kept in a community aviary we must not introduce new parakeets to the aviary during the breeding season. Experience has shown that newcomers are intensively and aggressively pursued during the breeding season. Victims of these aggressions are very likely to result. If a given couple housed in a breeding cage will not breed, it is a good idea to place another couple that will breed with them. They will set the right example!

LARGE PARAKEETS: Young lovebirds that have become independent should also be separated from their parents. The parents will wait until the fall,

Although cockatiels prefer to lay their eggs in a nest box, anxious birds will utilize any type of nesting container available.

need to watch out that they are not caught by other bird fanciers! If you have ringed your birds, you can at least prove that they are yours! Naturally, you cannot allow the young to fly loose very long—just for about four days—if you do not want to lose them. The young from the ringneck parakeet, turquoise parrot and Bourke's parrot to name a few, may not be used for breeding before they have reached the age of two years. For those who keep cockatiels we should keep an eye out for too closely related breedings. It is best, therefore, to swap your new young birds with fellow bird breeders. The offspring of the red-rumped parakeet should be separated from the parents once they have become independent, because the cock has the nasty habit of pursuing and attacking his children until they are dead. When the young have been removed from the parents, the hen will promptly start on a second clutch. All this also applies to the red-winged parrot and other similar species of hook-beaked birds. Young rosella species should be disturbed as little as possible initially, because they are very nervous in the beginning and constantly fly up against the wire or woodwork with quite a thud when alarmed. It would be no surprise to find that a bird(s) had broken its wing or leg from these collisions. If we disturb them as little as possible during the first few weeks, things will quickly improve.

WILD BIRDS: Once the young birds are ready to take flight, we again close the aviary door (see previous month). When they have become independent they should

however, before starting on a second round, although if we have a wet summer they will sometimes continue then. We must allow nature to take its course and not unduly rush matters. Young monk parakeets enjoy flying around in the garden with father. However, caution is our watchword! You see, these birds love to gnaw at the branches and twigs of fruit trees and your neighbors may not be so amused with that; you would also be separated from their parents. The parents are then likely to begin on another round; the care and procedure of course parallel that which we have already discussed.

CANARIES: At this time of the year your canaries will probably be busy with their last brood. For some it may be the second round; for others it may be the third. Bird fanciers who have canaries that started rather late and are busy with their second round may be tempted to allow the birds to begin yet another round. I strongly advise against this,

handling. What we have said in the previous months of course should still be adhered to. Although the nests have had good use and the young do not return to them at night any more, we should still not discard them just yet. First we will have to determine whether the hen is showing any signs of wanting to start a new brood. If this is the case—it would not be that exceptional if our tropical birds come to breed in the aviary more than once in a season—then we can clean up the old nest a little and provide a little new nesting

because any offspring that result are generally behind in everything. They often remain smaller than their older brothers and sisters, their feathering is less abundant, they go into the molt rather late, and they often take longer to attain their coloring (if they are color canaries). In the year that follows, the breeding results from those latecomers are usually poor.

JULY
EXOTICS: We could really be brief this month: July and August do not pose any special problems and do not require any special

Melba Finches (Pytilia melba) being hand fed with the use of a syringe.

material for our bird to add to her nest. Most birds will be very pleased with this. If you see that the hen intends to build a completely new nest it is best to remove the old one from the aviary, unless you have red-eared waxbills, aurora waxbills, Wiener's waxbills, etc., which make a grateful use of old nests.

ZEBRA FINCHES: Good exhibition birds are attained only through a strict continuous selective process and playing Cupid with a great deal of care and attention to details. Providing our zebra finch couples are in excellent health, we need not worry too much about their offspring, although it can happen that a 'runt' is found in an otherwise good brood. Needless to say, we pay close attention to coloring and marking. We cannot just combine a few colors. We would end up with a mishmash bird population, and we are sure not to want that. The young from this year must be placed according to individual colors. Our records should be carefully kept and properly updated, as we mentioned earlier. When selling young birds this will pay off for both the buyer and the seller. After all, you will be able to guarantee certain characteristics;

Damp environments should be avoided when keeping Black-crowned Waxbill (Estrilda nonnula).

the buyer will know he is not buying a cat in a bag. Perhaps there are couples that are in their second, third or perhaps even fourth year.

Since there are still other birds breeding in a community aviary, you cannot yet undertake an extensive 'spring' cleaning. It would be wise, however, to clean the old nest of the zebra finch couple a little. Also give them some building material (grass, sisal and hay). You already know that the parents deposit all of their offsprings droppings onto the edge of the nest. By giving them somewhat flexible nesting material a certain amount of ventilation is guaranteed. And anyone who has seen an old zebra finch nest will agree that this is no luxury. After having supplied them with new nesting material, then, we can follow the same routine as described in the prior months.

BUDGERIGARS: To guarantee a proper color heritability we will need to adhere to strict selection and excellent breeding pairs. I do not find it objectionable to house more than one couple in an aviary. But you should remember that they must all be identical in coloring and markings, because budgerigars are polygamous—in other words, the males will court and mate with every hen, given the opportunity. Another point I would like to make is that once in a while there will be some hens that just will not come to breed well and, in fact, disturb the nests of fellow species in an obnoxious manner and may even peck at the eggs or kill the young. A budgerigar breeder once wrote to me that a few of his hens had strong cannibalistic tendencies; they actually went into the nests of other fellow species, dragged out the young and made a hearty meal of them on the aviary floor. Obviously, such birds are totally unsuitable for breeding. They should be housed separately and not be given the chance to breed because experience has shown that these birds never achieve good breeding results anyway. We would also like to remind you, once again, that no new specimens should be placed in an aviary where parakeets are in the process of breeding.

LARGE PARAKEETS: Since the hatching period of these birds can take quite a long time, we should pay special attention to see that their nutritional requirements are fully met. Refresh their water frequently (perhaps adding a few drops of a proper disinfectant), provide them with a clean sand bath and spray them with lukewarm water every other day. Don't forget greens and fruit!

CANARIES: Since in most cases no new young birds are expected any more at this point in time, the bird breeder will, no doubt, have counted the young and estimated the profits! However, although the chicks have hatched, don't count on them too definitely yet! It can still happen, at this early stage, that lively young that were still fluttering around in flight in the evening and were arguing with each other lay dead the next morning, for no apparent reasons. We provided good food, fresh drinking water constantly, everything was kept nice and clean, and now we do not understand what went wrong. I am often asked for explanations, but I am afraid I don't have the answer either. There are still

inexplicable cases of deaths in the canary hobby. Mid-July is the time when we must take steps to protect our birds from the danger of mosquitoes. We know that mosquitoes can be carriers of the much dreaded disease canary pox—which is extremely contagious. If any of the

Violet-eared Waxbill
(Uraeginthus granatina)

droppings of an infected bird (which is generally doomed to die) land in the water dish, then we can rely on the fact that all our birds will be infected. It has happened more than once that out of a collection of, say, 100 healthy birds, only three or four survived. The only protection we can offer against mosquitoes is to completely cover the flight with a fine wire screen, and just to be sure, place a pair of white-eyes or an ordinary house and garden variety finch among your canaries. These 'guest birds' are fiery mosquito catchers and no mosquito that perchance enters the aviary, perhaps through a crack in the door, will escape from their hunting skills. During

Blue-capped Cordonbleu
(*Uraeginthus cyanocephala)*

the period that mosquitoes are abundant, it is also a good idea to give the birds cooled off boiled water, refreshing this perhaps once more during the day. I repeat: be sure not to wait too long before putting up the mesh screen.

AUGUST
As far as the details regarding this month's bird care are concerned, I would refer you to what was written for the months of June and July. What applies to one summer month pretty well applies to another. There are, however, two things to which I would like to draw extra attention: 1) lice control, and 2) formation of weed supply. Even though lice plague those breeders that are not very meticulous about cleanliness and hygiene the entire summer, this month they are definitely at their worst. Because of unhindered breeding upon breeding, lice colonies have sprung up here and there and grown to countless numbers. It is now definitely the time to step in and do something about it. Your bird dealer will no doubt carry several insecticides that are safe for birds.

Now that the young birds are pretty much independent, you can easily vacate cage upon cage or aviaries and flights to give them an extra turn. Don't be stingy with the insecticide; be sure not to miss any nook, crack or cranny!— not only inside the cage or aviary, but also right around it. For their size, lice can travel amazing distances to ensure themselves of a safe hiding place.

If your birds are kept indoors, be sure to look behind any pictures or anything else you may have hanging along the wall where the aviary or cage is kept. Catching the lice colonies at this time of year allows you to come as close to eradicating them as possible. It is best to take care of this job during the day, because they are then in their hiding places and usually not on the birds.

As far as the second subject is concerned (weeds), this month is the best time to collect weeds to store for the winter, because in no other month are they growing in such profusion as in August, everywhere you look. Just as the farmer stores hay to feed his stock during the winter, we should collect and store bunches and bunches of weeds that we can hang up in the aviary throughout the winter. Pick as much as you can as long as it can be dried (not chickweed), such as plantain (*Plantago*), grass seed, common ragwort, shepherd's purse, etc. Make up easy-to-handle bunches and tie a string around each one. Then hang them perhaps from a rafter in a shed, a garage or the attic. If you gather some 50 or 60 of these bunches, you will be able to hang them in your aviary at a rate of one bunch three times a week for the entire period that fresh weed seeds are not available. Not only

these dried seeds, you can give your birds fresh chickweed for greens. These can be picked fresh practically throughout the entire year. It is only during a period of bitter frost that the stalk will die off. There are quite a few bird fanciers, however, who collect the pollens of chickweed, bring it to their own garden or some piece of unused nearby land and place a wooden window with glass on top of this little plantation; they may even add a little petroleum burner to keep their own little supply of 'greens' frost-free. With the right attitude and a little effort we can provide ideal care for our feathered friends.

SEPTEMBER

EXOTICS: Our tropical birds now also have the breeding period behind them. All nesting material

*Lavender Waxbills (*Estrilda caerulescens*) must be housed in spacious uncrowded aviaries to prevent their tendency toward feather plucking.*

are these dried weed seeds a (free) vitamin-rich food, but these bunches also provide the birds with something to do and a change of pace. In addition to

must be removed from the aviary and the young taken away from their parents, if this has not already been done. All of our 'small' stock can be brought indoors into their winter abode at the beginning of October (if the weather is still nice). I know there are several species that can be kept outdoors during the winter, but experience has shown, nevertheless, that the winter months claim quite a few casualties.

Because September/October is also the molting period, we must be sure not to forget cod-liver oil. In addition, it would be very good if we have dried ant eggs and other insects to give them. Extra soaked bread (preferably soaked in milk) is also good at this time. If possible we now separate the cocks and the hens. In the meantime you can start making selections among your young birds. Swap birds with other fanciers so that when the next breeding season comes you will be able to start with unrelated couples.

ZEBRA FINCHES: September is of course too late to still allow your zebra finches to breed, because this would only result in egg binding and in inferior young. This is also the time to think about our big, major cleaning. We no longer provide any nesting material, and we add three drops of cod-liver oil to one kilo of seed for the upcoming fall and molt.

Now that the breeding season is at its end, we must start making our selections. A wise zebra finch breeder will be sure to keep his best birds himself. This does not mean that he should quickly sell his 'runts.' Nevertheless, it is better to get rid of them, but if we are good breeders, the number of birds that are somewhat inferior will not be so great.

BUDGERIGARS: Those budgies that we would like to take to the bird shows must, of course, first comply with form and color requirements. This is not the time or place for us to delve into all these details, which, incidentally, are fully covered in *Breeding Budgerigars* by the same author (T.F.H. Publications, Inc.). We would, however, like to discuss the details of preparing your parakeets for a show. For one thing, if we start with the preparation early enough, we will save ourselves a lot of trouble. A parakeet is very smart and can learn quickly. Show parakeets will have to become accustomed to show cages. In most cases the parakeets have been reared in roomy breeding cages or aviaries which offered them a lot of space for movement. It is best to now place the birds in question in breeding cages; each bird gets his own cage. I am sure it is unnecessary at this point to add once more that these cages should be spotlessly clean and not too small, since our show birds must also be clean when they come to the examiners' table. With a little river sand on the bottom, which we replace regularly, we await the molt. A little cod-liver oil can do a lot to

White-throated Finch
(*Sporophila albigularis*)

help them through this period without any undue problems. The perches must be situated in such a way so that the bird's tail does not scrape against the ground. About fourteen days before the budgerigars are to go to the exhibition, we place them in the little show cages.

LARGE PARAKEETS: September is the time for the big cleaning. The perches for our larger parakeet varieties will have to be replaced. The Jandaya conure, for example, is likely to do such a job on his perch that there is no doubt it will need replacing. We should remember that the ringneck parakeet needs fresh twigs and branches for gnawing during the winter and fall as well. Providing these birds have a really good wind- and frost-free night shelter, they can spend the winter outdoors. I am mentioning this now before your big cleaning. The night shelter must be livable—so wind- and frost-free. If this is definitely the case, I see no reason why our large parakeet varieties cannot stay outdoors during the winter months. It is best to bring our lovebirds indoors into winter quarters at the beginning of October.

WILD BIRDS: It is likely that your wild birds will become somewhat restless toward the fall; their migratory instincts are waking up. This is why it is best to separate them from any tropical birds, etc. Many of our wild birds can also stay outdoors, providing again, that the night shelter is satisfactory.

CANARIES: Some of our canaries are already molting at this time; others will follow shortly. Be sure that their menu leaves nothing to be desired,

Diamond Firetail
(Emblema guttata)

especially at this time. So in addition to the usual seed mixes, give plenty of strength foods, cuttlebone, grit and greens, preferably chickweed. We must be especially careful to guard against drafts during the molting period, because young birds in particular are very sensitive to drafts during this period. More than once breeders will lose their most beautiful young during the molt. Everything is blamed, from the cock's chromosomes to the seed mix, but in actual fact, we forgot to close the door when the window was already open, and these causes are often overlooked.

OCTOBER

There are no special points to keep in mind for October; it is enough to follow the care

Both male and female European Goldfinch are similar in coloration.

prescribed in the previous months. Because the nights are already long, our birds must do without water and food for long stretches of time. I have never had a problem with hungry or thirsty birds when I made their day longer by using lights. In the evening I would leave the light on until 9 o'clock (and then gradually let it go out with the use of a dimmer switch), and in the morning the light went on from 6 o'clock until there was sufficient sunlight. Timers will greatly simplify this task for you. When the days are extra dark with bad weather, you may need to switch your lights on sooner.

Canaries can be kept outside if the aviary is situated in a protected location and is made for the most part with glass or plastic panels. This applies, in the first place, to the top side, so that no rain or snow can cover the bottom of the aviary. The bottom must remain dry. Canary feet are very sensitive to moisture, which can cause so-called calcified feet and cause the condition of the bird to deteriorate sharply. The safest way to bring these birds through the winter—and this is true for all of our feathered friends with only a few exceptions—is to house them in a dry, light, unheated attic. It is perfectly all right to keep the cocks and hens together until February starts.

We should start deciding now which birds we want to keep and which we want to sell. But more about this in the month of November.

NOVEMBER

EXOTICS: In some areas a great many tropical birds are dyed at this time—with the holiday season almost upon us—so caution is our watchword. Well-known exotic birds such as the red-eared waxbills, red avadavats (watch out: these are hot favorites for 'touching up' with a little extra color), munias, spice birds, gold-breasted waxbills (here again this species is also often 'painted' and then sold under the most fanciful names. Bengalese, silverbills, gray singing finches, etc., are often sold for very high prices. If we keep a sharp eye out for their health and the general impression they make, we will not have to feel 'taken' later; we may end up with a bird that turns out to be colored differently than when we bought it, but at least it is healthy—and you were warned! You are always better off buying your birds from a trusted and knowledgeable bird merchant. The time for the bird shows is almost upon us.

ZEBRA FINCHES: It is best to shop around at this time if you are looking for good buys. Beginners are best off starting with a couple of pure heritable (homozygous) gray zebra finches. It is important to get birds that

Swee Waxbill
(Estrilda melanotis melanotis)

are in excellent health; they must not be dirty or have their heads stuck in their feathers, sleeping on a perch or in some corner of the aviary. They must have clear eyes and a smooth plumage.

GRASS FINCHES: At this time there are also quite a few Australian finches offered for sale. I am thinking in particular of various parrot finches and waxbills. No doubt you are aware that you should be cautious particularly when buying the more expensive species, because it happens quite often that the less-than-excellent specimens are 'touched up' with aniline or other dyes.

These birds that are very sensitive to temperature changes are best not purchased at the shows, since we cannot know the circumstances of their transportation. It is wiser to wait a few weeks after the birds are back home with their owner and then go to him to negotiate. We will do best by doing business with trusted dealers who keep their birds at a constant temperature. The same usually also applies to the more expensive tropical insect-eaters.

BUDGERIGARS: Actually, we could repeat the same thing for our budgies. Interested parties have a wide range to choose from at this time. I would advise against starting with the more difficult colors. The more common colors (green, blue) are also less expensive. I would advise, however, to watch out for pure heritability, good form and such. Then we cannot go wrong.

In conclusion, here is a good tip: with Christmas not very far off, why don't you plan on giving your children a couple of little hook-beaked friends in a fairly roomy cage that has horizontal bars? When we involve our youngsters with pets early in life, we will be rearing real friends of Nature. And real 'friends of Nature' are also good for their fellow man!

Masked Firefinch
(Lagonosticta larvata)

Virginian Cardinal
*(*Richmondena cardinalis*)*

LARGE PARAKEETS: These are now regularly offered for sale, and sometimes at very reasonable prices. Generally, they are selected birds that are a pleasure to behold! Nevertheless, I would advise you to take along an expert before buying any birds. Experience has taught us that sometimes 'reconditioned' birds are offered for sale—that is to say birds that are actually a few years old but which have had their worst 'faults' camouflaged by special hyped-up feeds; the next molt, however, or even simply normal care, will bring these 'faults' back to light. Look closely at the beak, feet and large feathers of the wings and tail. The coloring seen on the whole is also important. The colors must be clear and the feathers should be shiny. Dull colors mean either old or unhealthy birds.

CANARIES: The sale and resale of canaries is at its peak at this time of year. The buyers can be divided into two groups: the breeder/fancier, and the private individual. Breeders of both song and color canaries can best buy colored canaries bred in the current year (complete with examiner's approval slip). We are then safe, at least, with song canary cocks and color canary hens. The latter pass on the color they reveal, although the cocks do not necessarily do so. If we buy cocks, then we need to be assured that they are pure heritable, for which we need a guarantee from a trusted dealer. If we take a chance and buy a cock just anywhere, then it should not surprise us if we end up with a potpourri of colors, including even pied birds. Pied birds and others not suitable for breeding are nonetheless not worthless as far as resale is concerned. If we place a small ad in a local paper in which we offer lively, singing cocks, you will be surprised how many private individuals will come to buy a singing cage bird.

DECEMBER

In the previous months we have given you various tips regarding the housing of your birds during the winter, and the buying of them. There is one thing I would still like to point out: specifically, do not place birds near a heater

Birds in outdoor aviaries must be checked often during the winter months.

after they have been exposed to cold for some time (such as during transportation). It is very dangerous to do this without giving them a chance to become acclimated. Catching cold and even worse results can develop. In fact, it can have a fatal outcome. Bird bones are primarily filled with air. By exposing the bird to sudden heat, the air expands and puts an enormous amount of tension in the bird's body. Birds often die in excruciating pain as a result. Sudden temperature changes, both up and down, are extremely dangerous for all birds.

In conclusion, a pointer for winter breeders. (Although I am not in favor of this, in fact I personally object to it, we cannot completely disregard those that like to do this or simply cannot stop doing it.) As far as the large parakeets are concerned, the only chance of success they may have is when the birds in question are housed in a roomy aviary and have not bred during the summer. Otherwise the hens become too run-down, which will be reflected in the birds as well as in the offspring. The same applies to canaries. I would also add that young canaries must be at least ten months old before we allow them to breed. If we get young birds during the winter, we will have to provide them with a constant room temperature and provide them with a partially artificial day, as described before. The birds must have light from 5 a.m. to 10:30 p.m.; otherwise nothing will come of these already risky ventures.

THE COMPLETE CAGE AND AVIARY BIRD HANDBOOK
by David Alderton (H-1087)

Treating the species by family, this work provides current information on the following seed-eating birds: canaries and other selected fringillids; all the commonly available estrildid finches, with details on Zebra and Society finches; many of the whydahs and weaver finches; a sampling of the buntings and tanagers; pigeons and quails. The psittacine sections cover Budgerigars, Cockatiels, Lovebirds and their varieties, along with a representative collection of other species. Less usual avicultural subjects are species from these groups: barbets, hornbills, toucans, bulbuls, leafbirds, babblers, thrushes, white-eyes, sunbirds, hummingbirds, mynahs, starlings, crows, and touracos. Each section contains remarks about feeding, followed by species commentaries. Opening with a chapter on avian biology, subsequent chapters cover birds as pets and generally discuss housing, feeding, management, illness, breeding, and the genetics of the color mutations. Drawings and photos help the reader to visualize anatomical structures, the design of aviaries and furnishings, and the paradigms of inheritance.

Illustrated with 167 color and 20 black and white photos and more than 60 drawings. Hard cover, 7½ × 9½", 160 pp.

BREEDING BIRDS AT HOME
by Jurgen Nicolai (H-1038)

This book provides a general discussion of bird husbandry and the breeding cycle from start to finish. Included are many practical suggestions about nesting material, preferences of certain groups of birds, and relations between parents and young.

Illustrated with 141 color and 28 black and white photos. Hard cover, 5½ × 8", 160 pp.

BUILDING AN AVIARY
by Prof. Carl Naether and Dr. Matthew M. Vriends (PS-763)

This excellent how-to book offers practical suggestions and step-by-step instructions for equipping and constructing an aviary to suit the needs and tastes of the individual fancier. Written for all birdkeepers, beginners and veterans alike, whether their interest is for fun or profit. Gives excellent information about which species are compatible.

Illustrated with 50 color and 38 black and white photos. Hard cover, 5½ × 8", 160 pp.

BIRD DISEASES: An Introduction to the Study of Birds in Health and Disease
by Drs. L. Arnall and I. F. Keymer (H-964)

Highly specialized book. Written for bird pathologists and bird dealers. It requires a thorough education in biology to be understood, but experienced bird lovers can recognize symptoms and diseases from the many illustrations and thus be able to treat their own birds. Recommended for scientific libraries only.

INDEX

CO-004 S

AVIARIES
A COMPLETE INTRODUCTION

—Dr. Matthew M. Vriends—

Cuban Finch (Tiaris canora)